RECORDED VERSIONS GUITAR

AUTHENTIC TRANSCRIPTIONS
WITH NOTES AND TABLATURE

blink-182 GREATEST HITS

ISBN 978-1-4234-0979-3

HAL•LEONARD®
CORPORATION

7777 W. BLUEMOUND RD. P.O. BOX 13819 MILWAUKEE, WI 53213

Visit Hal Leonard Online at
www.halleonard.com

Carousel

Words and Music by Scott Raynor, Mark Hoppus and Tom De Longe

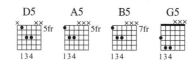

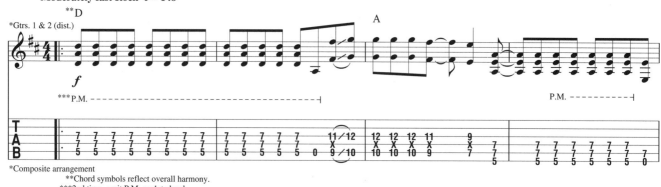

*Composite arrangement
**Chord symbols reflect overall harmony.
***2nd time, omit P.M. on 1st chord.

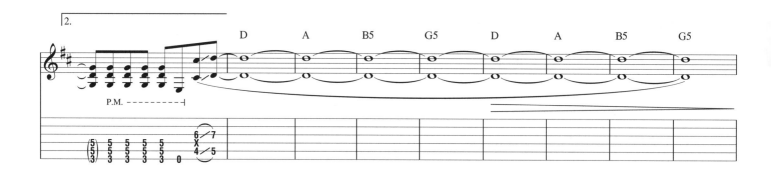

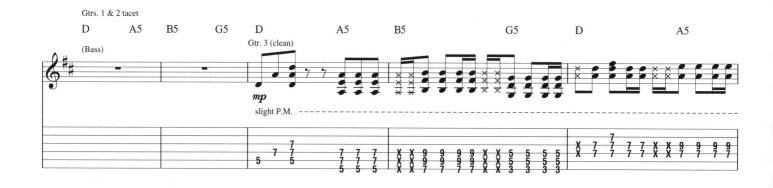

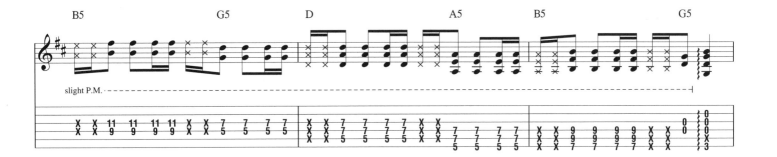

Faster ♩ = 208
Double-time feel

Gtr. 3 tacet

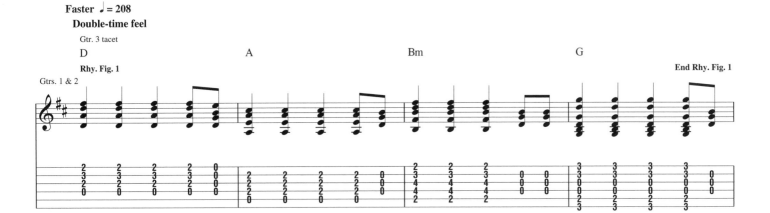

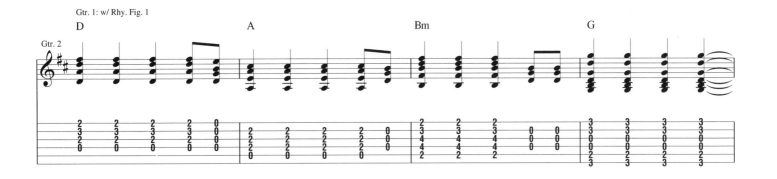

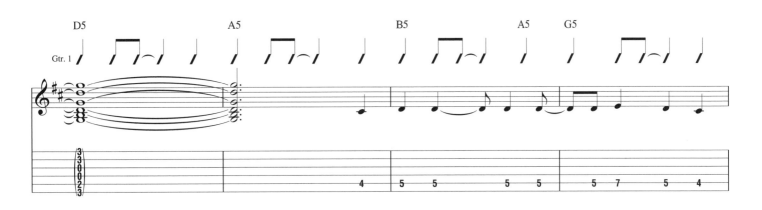

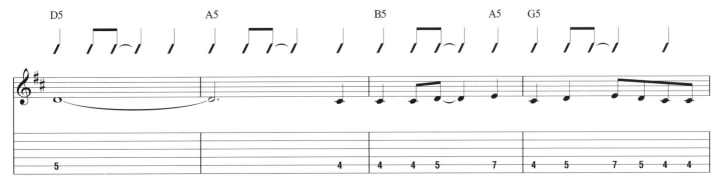

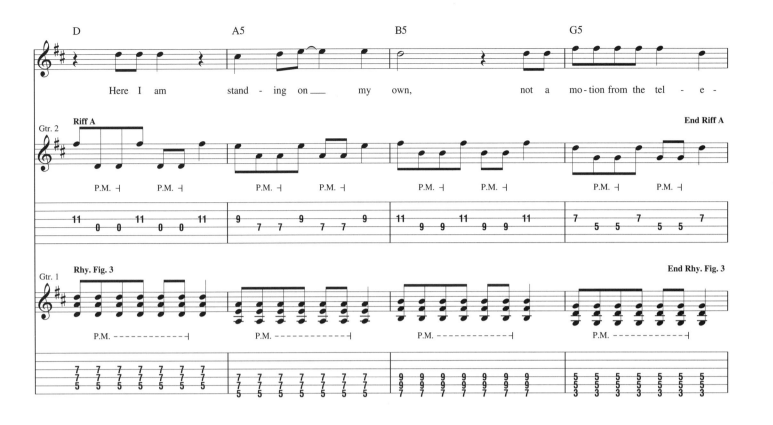

Here I am stand-ing on ___ my own, not a mo-tion from the tel - e -

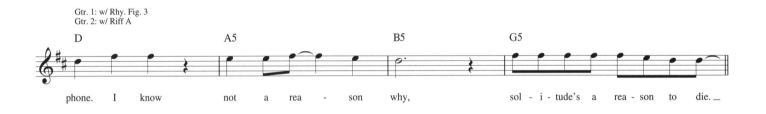

Gtr. 1: w/ Rhy. Fig. 3
Gtr. 2: w/ Riff A

phone. I know not a rea-son why, sol-i-tude's a rea-son to die. ___

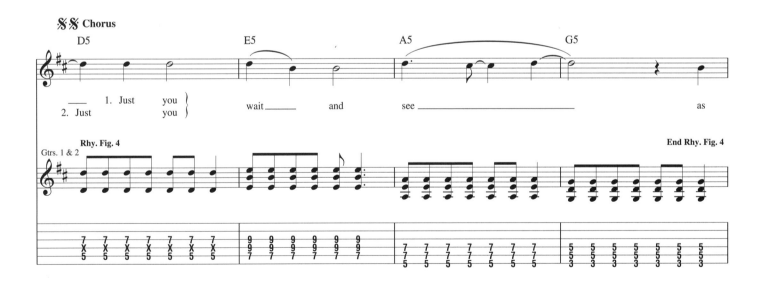

§§ **Chorus**

1. Just you
2. Just you
wait ___ and see ___ as

Gtrs. 1 & 2: w/ Rhy. Fig. 4 (2 times)

school life is ___ a, it is a wok-en ___ dream. ___

Aren't you _feel-ing_ a - _lone?_

To Coda 2 ⊕   _D.S. al Coda 1_

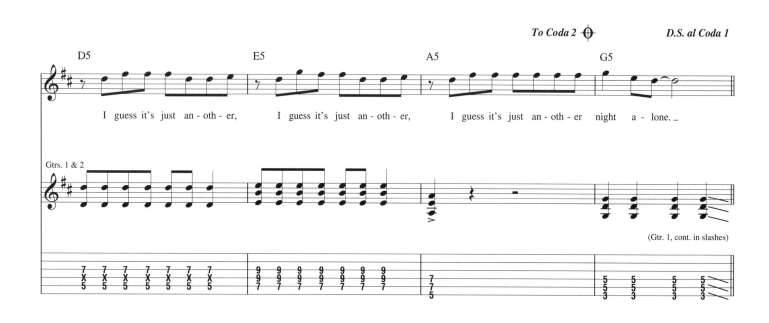

I guess it's just an-oth-er,   I guess it's just an-oth-er,   I guess it's just an-oth-er night a - lone. _

Gtrs. 1 & 2

(Gtr. 1, cont. in slashes)

⊕ **Coda 1**

Bridge

End double-time feel

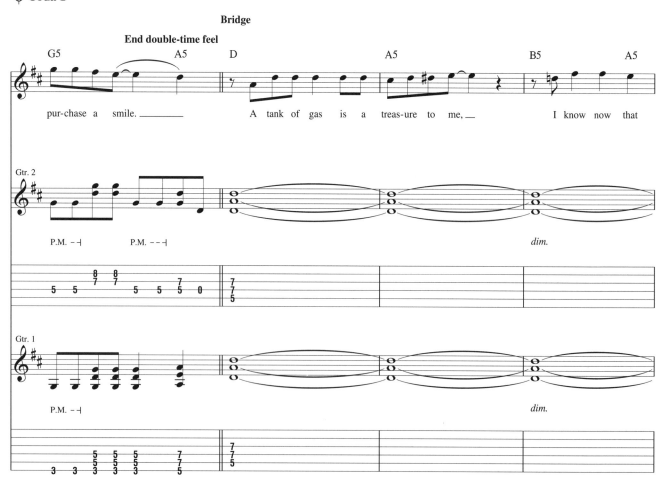

pur-chase a smile. _____   A tank of gas is a treas-ure to me, —   I know now that

Gtr. 2

P.M. ---| P.M. ---| _dim._

Gtr. 1

P.M. ---| _dim._

noth-ing is free. _____ I talk to you ev-'ry now and then, _ I nev-er felt so a-lone a-gain.

Gtrs. 1 & 2

(Gtr. 1, cont. in slashes)

Interlude

Gtr. 1

(cont. in notation)

Riff B

End Riff B

Gtr. 2

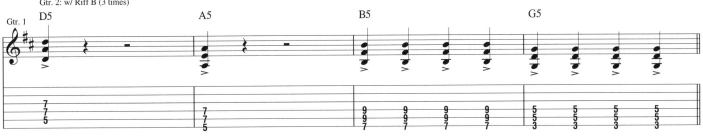

Gtr. 2: w/ Riff B (3 times)

Gtr. 1

2nd time, D.S.S. al Coda 2

Double-time feel

Coda 2

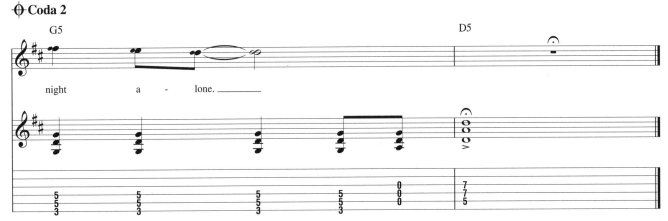

night a - lone. _____

M&M

Words and Music by Scott Raynor, Mark Hoppus and Tom De Longe

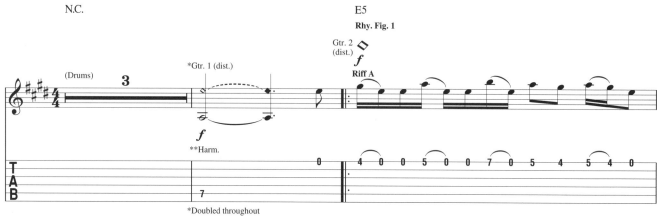

Intro
Fast Rock ♩ = 168
Double-time feel

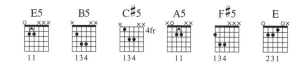

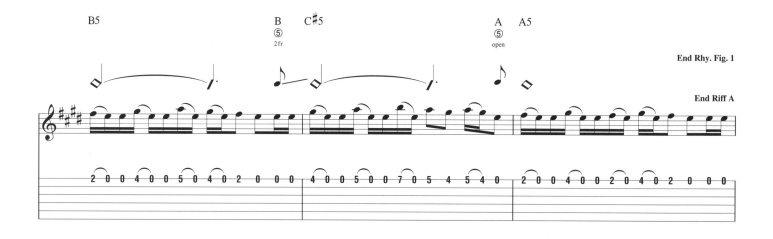

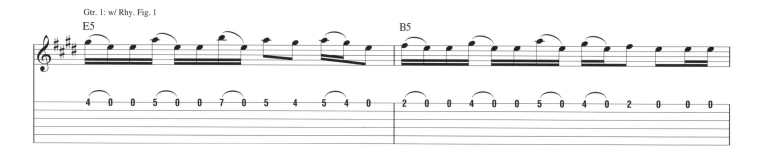

Verse

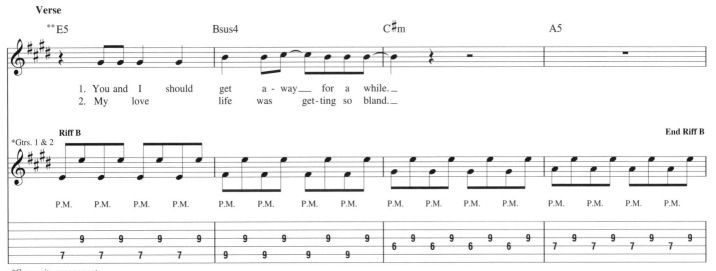

E5   **Bsus4**   **C#m**   **A5**

1. You and I should get a-way___ for a while.___
2. My love life was get-ting so bland.___

Riff B   **End Riff B**

*Gtrs. 1 & 2

P.M. P.M. P.M. P.M. P.M. P.M. P.M. P.M. P.M. P.M. P.M. P.M. P.M. P.M. P.M. P.M.

*Composite arrangement
     **Chord symbols reflect overall harmony.

Gtrs. 1 & 2: w/ Riff B

E5   **Bsus4**   **C#m**   **A5**

I just want to be a-lone ___ with your smile.
There are on-ly so man-y ways___ I can make love with my hand.

E5   **E5/B**   **E5/C#**   **A5**

Buy some can-dy and cig-a-rettes ___ and we'll get in ___ my car.
Some-times it makes me want___ to laugh.

Riff C   **End Riff C**

Gtrs. 1 & 2

let ring ---

Gtrs. 1 & 2: w/ Riff C

E5   **E5/B**   **E5/C#**   **A5**

We'll blast the ster-e-o _____ and we'll drive to Mad-a-gas-car.
Some-times I want to take ___ my toast-er in the bath.___

Be-cause when

Chorus

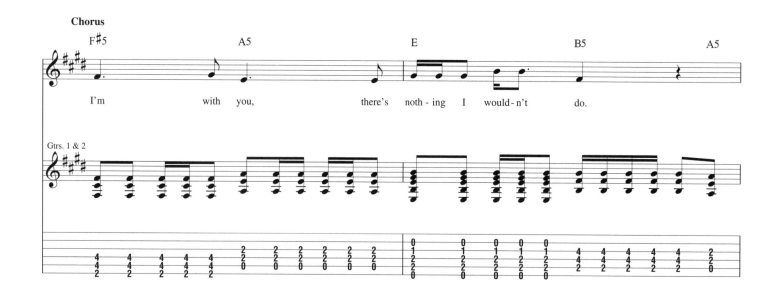

I'm with you, there's noth-ing I would-n't do.

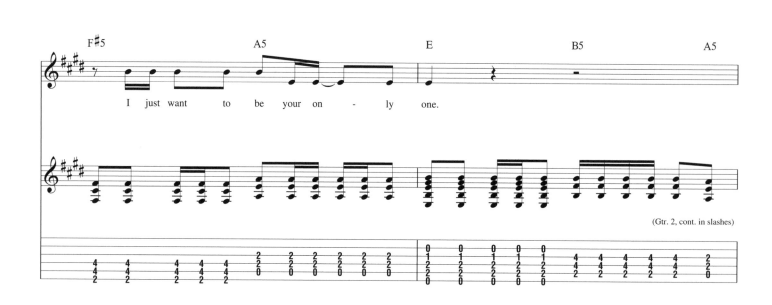

I just want to be your on - ly one.

(Gtr. 2, cont. in slashes)

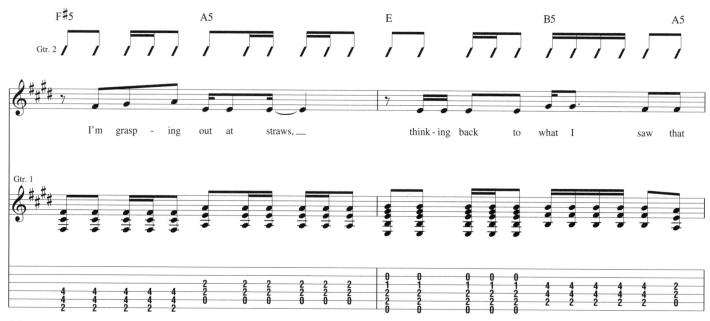

I'm grasp-ing out at straws, ___ think-ing back to what I saw that

10

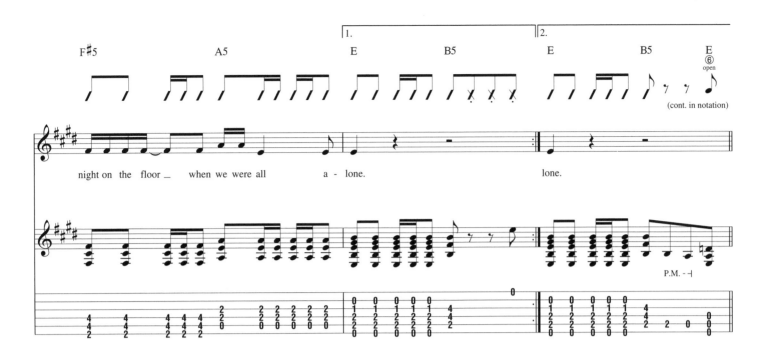

night on the floor ___ when we were all   a - lone.   lone.

(cont. in notation)

P.M.

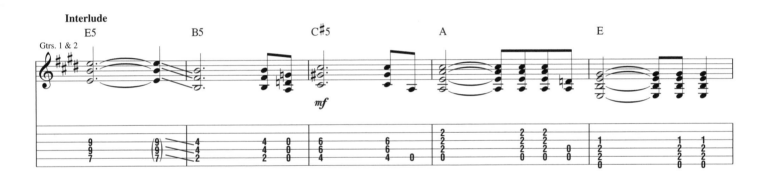

Interlude

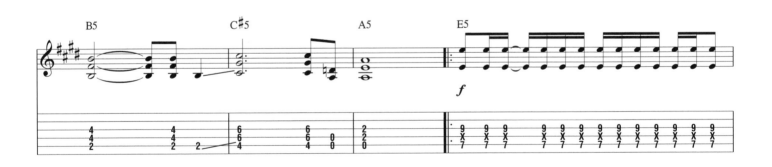

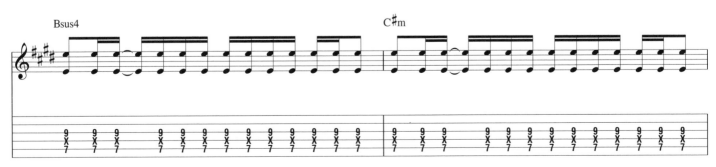

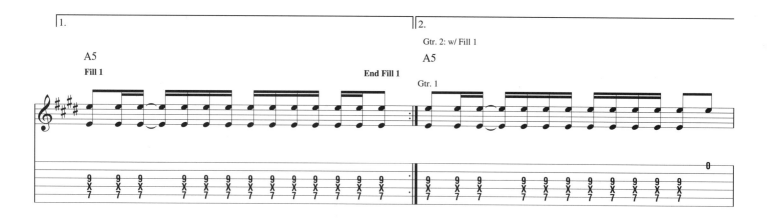

Outro

Gtr. 1: w/ Riff A (3 1/4 times)
Gtr. 2: w/ Rhy. Fig. 1 (4 times)

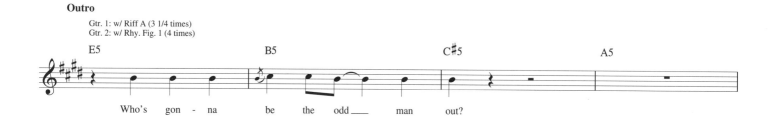

Who's gon - na be the odd man out?

I don't wan - na be the odd man out.

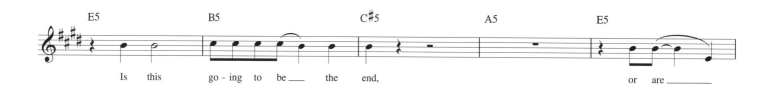

Is this go - ing to be the end, or are

you go - ing to be my new girl - friend?

Dammit

Words and Music by Scott Raynor, Mark Hoppus and Tom De Longe

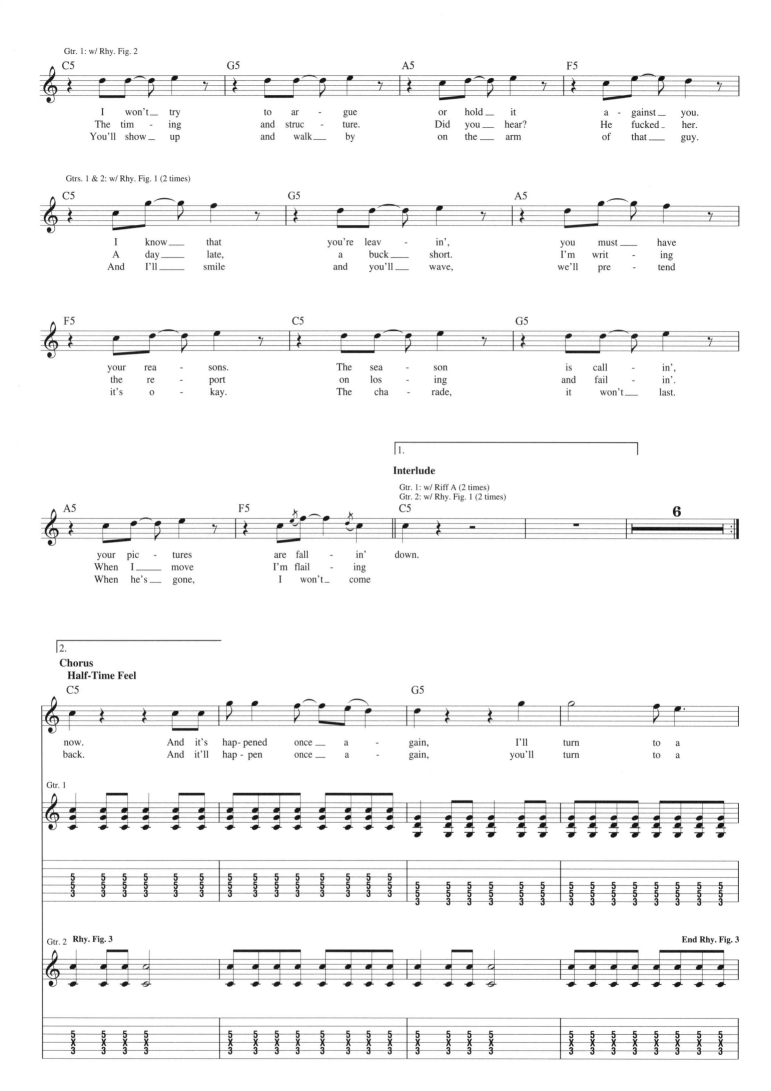

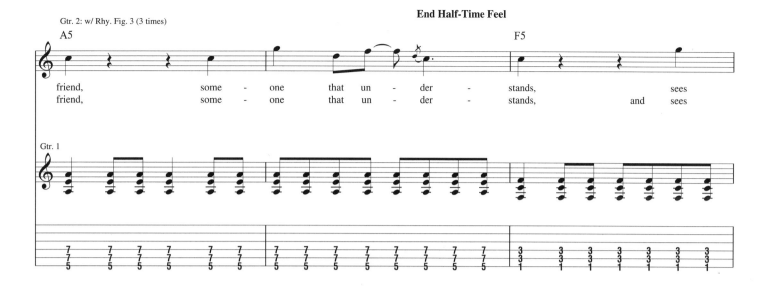

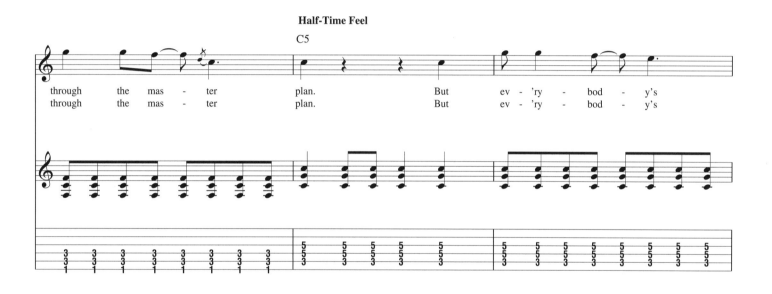

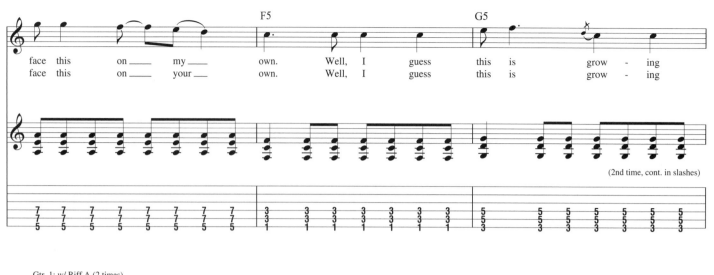

face this on ___ my ___ own. Well, I guess this is grow - ing
face this on ___ your ___ own. Well, I guess this is grow - ing

(2nd time, cont. in slashes)

Gtr. 1: w/ Riff A (2 times)
Gtr. 2: w/ Rhy. Fig. 1 (2 times)

up.   Well, I guess this is grow - ing

D.S. al Coda
(take 2nd ending)

up.

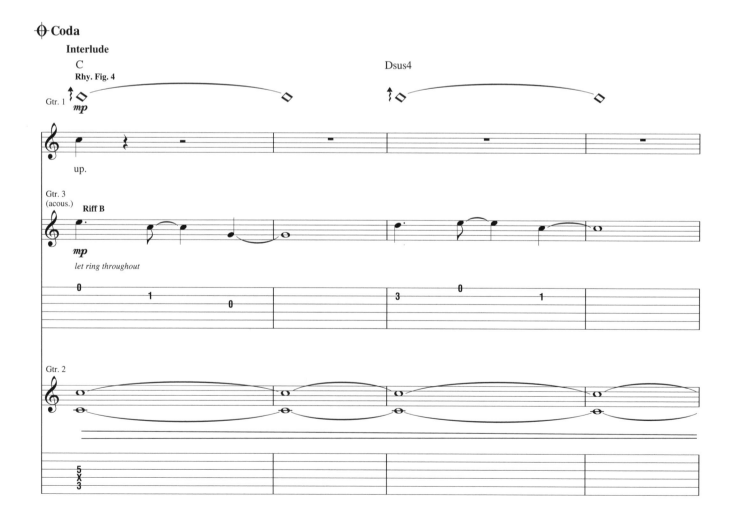

Coda

Interlude

up.

Gtr. 3
(acous.) **Riff B**

let ring throughout

Gtr. 2

16

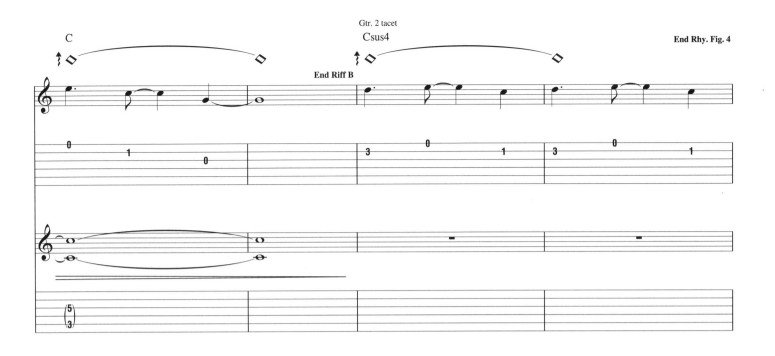

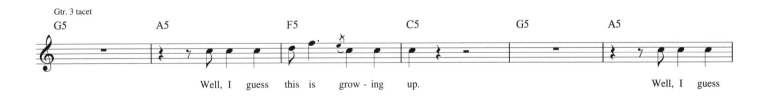

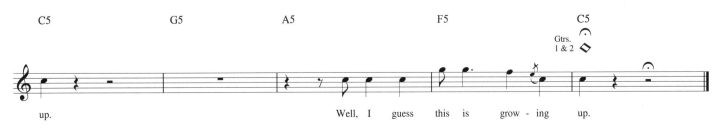

Josie

Words and Music by Scott Raynor, Mark Hoppus and Tom De Longe

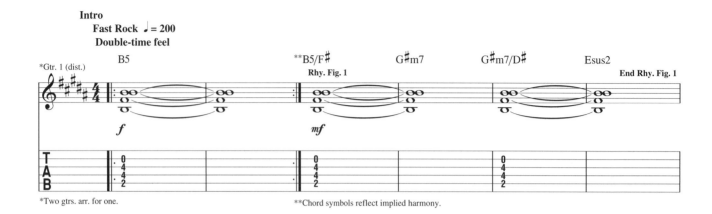

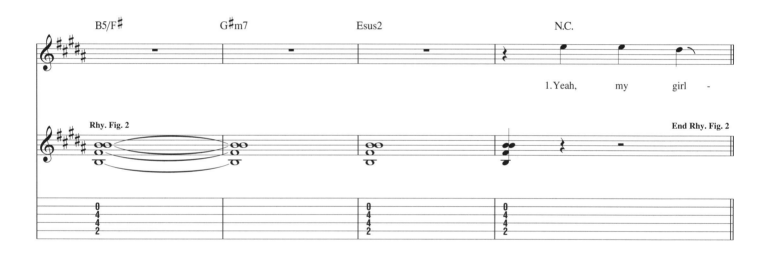

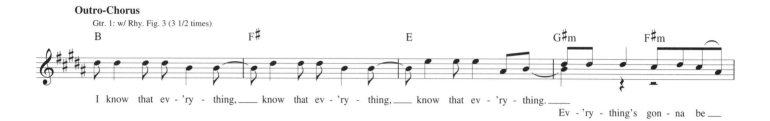

Outro-Chorus

Gtr. 1: w/ Rhy. Fig. 3 (3 1/2 times)

I know that ev - 'ry - thing,____ know that ev - 'ry - thing,____ know that ev - 'ry - thing.____ Ev - 'ry - thing's gon - na be____

I know that ev - 'ry - thing,____ know that ev - 'ry - thing,____ know that ev - 'ry - thing.____

fine. Ev - 'ry - thing's gon - na be____

I know that ev - 'ry - thing,____ know that ev - 'ry - thing,____ know that ev - 'ry - thing.____

fine.

____ Ev - 'ry - thing's gon - na be ____ fine.

I know that ev - 'ry - thing,____ know that ev - ry - thing,____

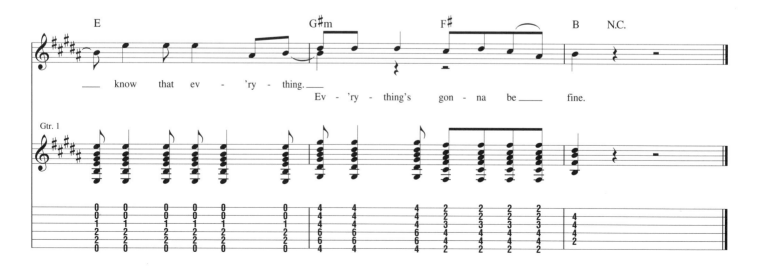

____ know that ev - 'ry - thing. Ev - 'ry - thing's gon - na be____ fine.

Gtr. 1

What's My Age Again?

Words and Music by Tom De Longe and Mark Hoppus

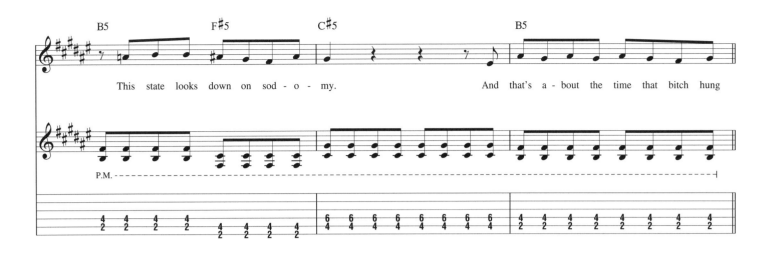

This state looks down on sod - o - my. And that's a - bout the time that bitch hung

Chorus
Gtr. 2: w/ Rhy. Fig. 1

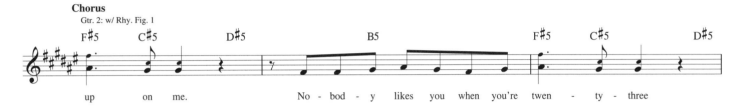

up on me. No - bod - y likes you when you're twen - ty - three

and are still more a - mused by prank phone calls. What the hell is call I - D? My

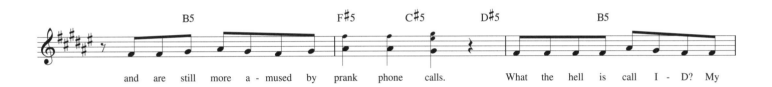

friends say I should act my age. What's my age a - gain? What's my age a - gain?

Interlude

Gtr. 2 tacet

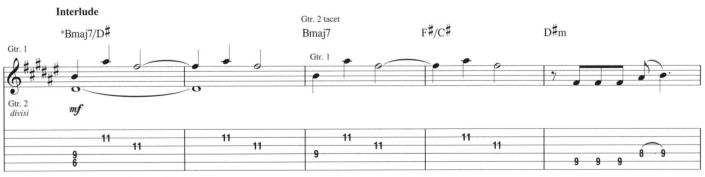

* Chord symbols reflect overall harmony.

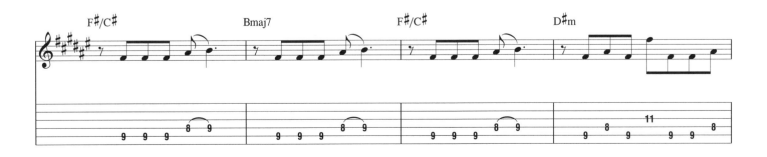

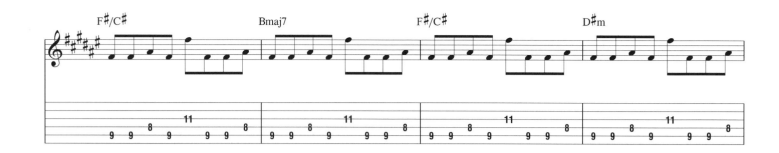

D.S. al Coda

And that's a - bout the time she walked a -

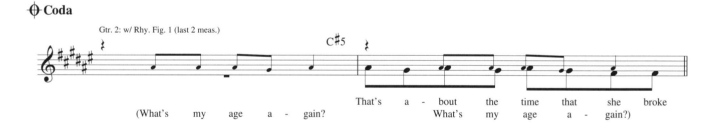

(What's my age a - gain?)

That's a - bout the time that she broke
What's my age a - gain?)

Chorus
Gtr. 2: w/ Rhy. Fig. 1

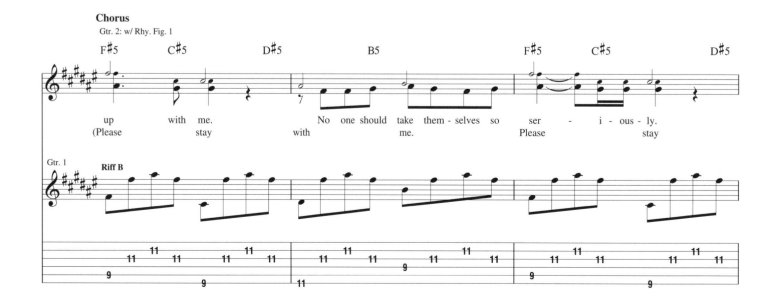

up with me.
(Please stay

with me.
No one should take them - selves so ser - i - ous - ly.
Please stay

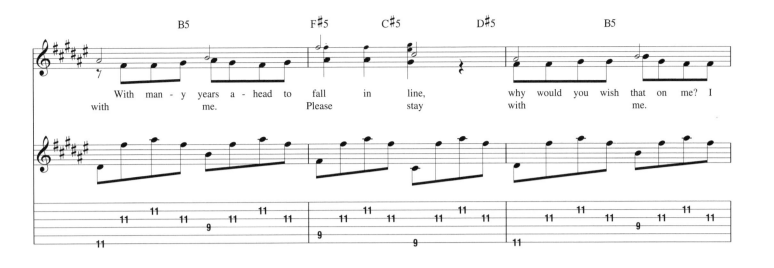

With man - y years a - head to fall in line, why would you wish that on me? I
with me. Please stay with me.

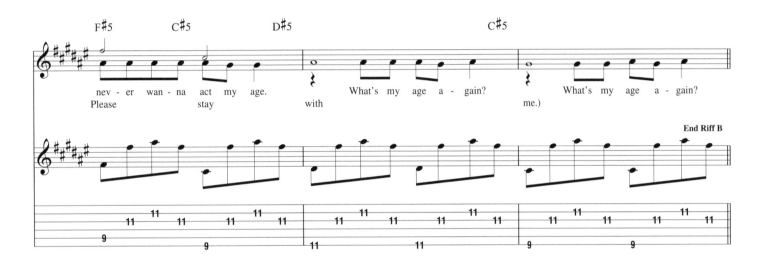

nev - er wan - na act my age. What's my age a - gain?
Please stay with What's my age a - gain?
me.)

End Riff B

Outro

Gtr. 1: w/ Riff B
Gtr. 2: w/ Rhy. Fig. 1

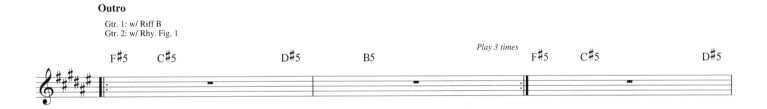

Play 3 times

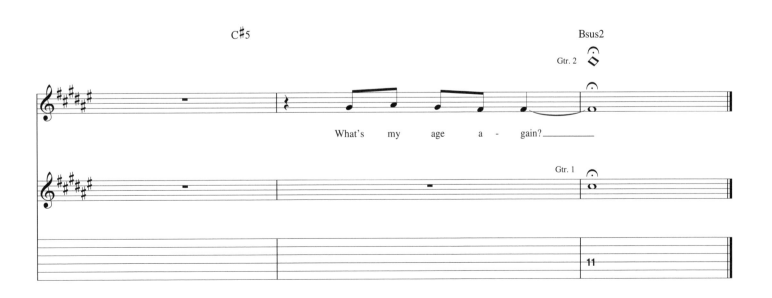

What's my age a - gain?

All the Small Things

Words and Music by Tom De Longe and Mark Hoppus

Verse

Gtr. 1: w/ Rhy. Fig. 2
Gtr. 2 tacet

2. Late night, come home. _____ Work sucks, I know.__

D.S. al Coda

Gtr. 1: w/ Rhy. Fig. 3

___ She left me ros - es by the stairs. __ Sur - pris - es let me know she cares. _

Coda

Interlude

Gtr. 1

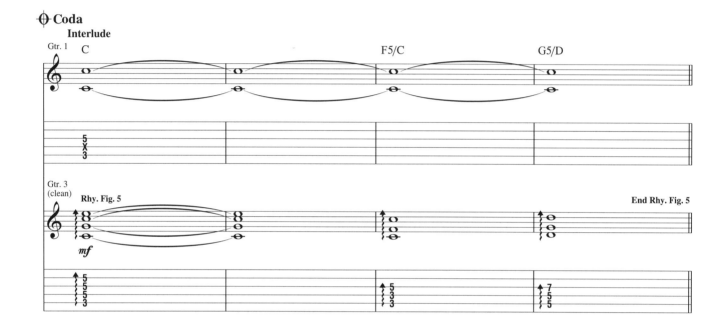

Gtr. 3: w/ Rhy. Fig. 5 (3 times)

Gtr. 1

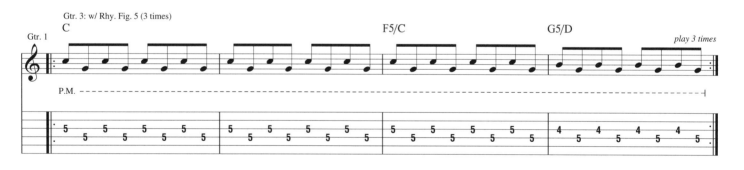

P.M. -

Outro

Gtr. 1: w/ Rhy. Fig. 4 (2 times)
Gtr. 2: w/ Riff A (3 1/2 times)

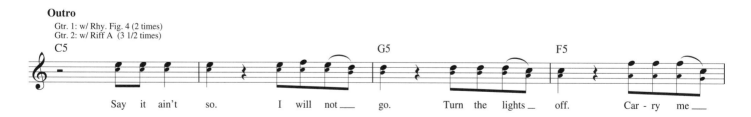

Say it ain't so. I will not __ go. Turn the lights __ off. Car - ry me __

home. Keep your head still. I'll be your _ thrill. The night will go __ on, my lit - tle wind -

30

Adam's Song

Words and Music by Tom De Longe and Mark Hoppus

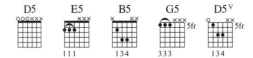

Gtrs. 1, 2, 3, & 5: Tune down 1 step:
(low to high) D-G-C-F-A-D

Gtr. 4: Drop D tuning, down 1 step:
(low to high) C-G-C-F-A-D

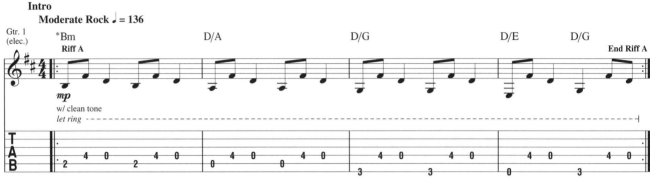

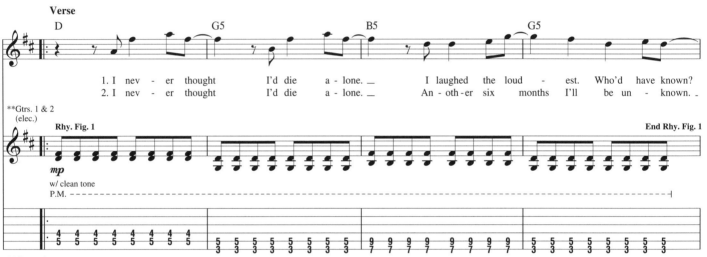

*Chord symbols reflect implied harmony.

G5   B5   G5

___   to   go   on.   You'll be   sor - ry   when   I'm___

___   in   the   hall? ___ Please be tell   Mom   this   is   not   her ___

Interlude

gone.
fault.

Chorus

3rd time, Gtrs. 1, 2 & 3: w/ Riffs B, B1 & B2 (2 times)
3rd time, Gtr. 4: w/ Rhy. Fig. 2 (2 times)

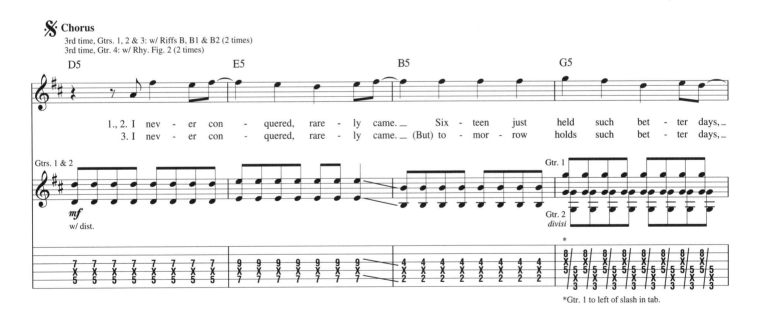

1., 2. I nev - er con - quered, rare - ly came. ___ Six - teen just held such bet - ter days, ___
3. I nev - er con - quered, rare - ly came. (But) to - mor - row holds such bet - ter days, ___

*Gtr. 1 to left of slash in tab.

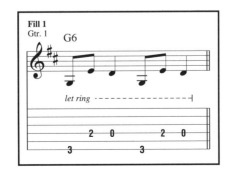

33

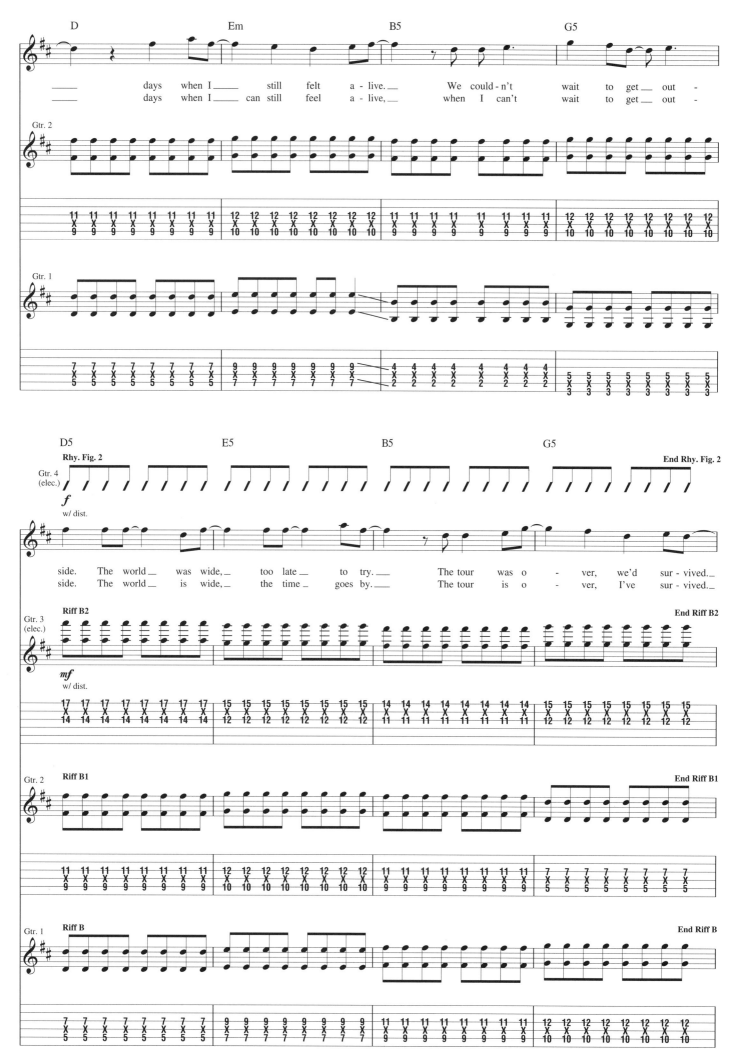

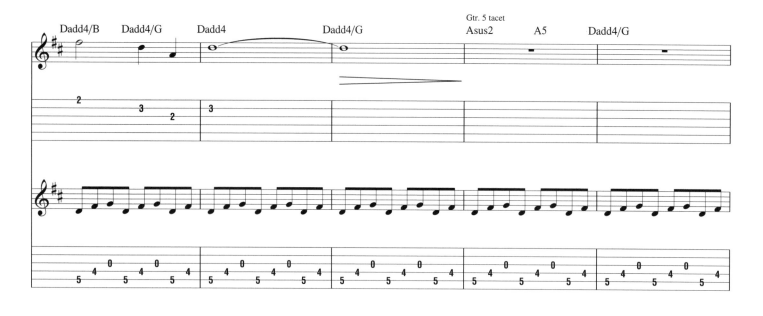

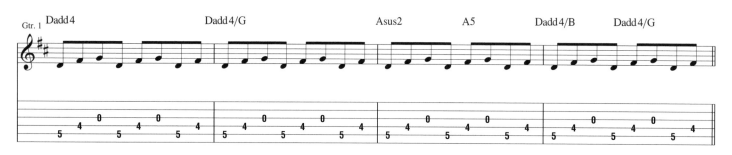

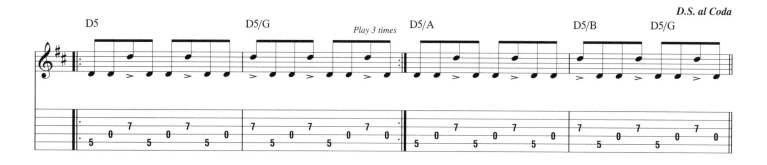

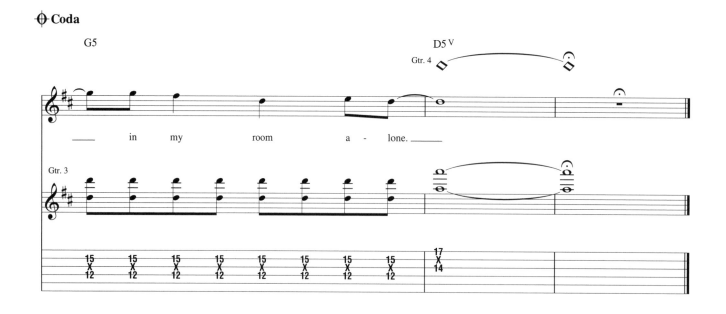

Man Overboard

Words and Music by Tom De Longe and Mark Hoppus

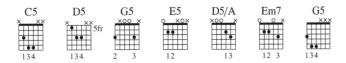

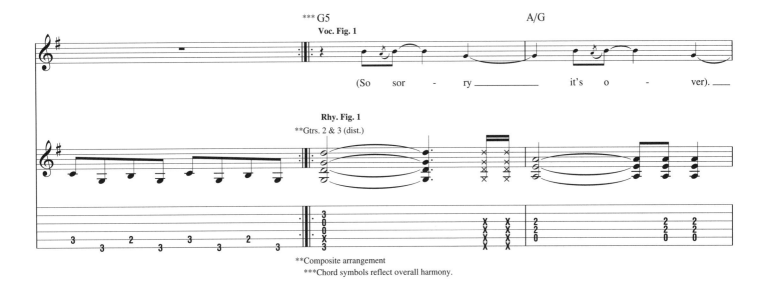

*Bass arr. for gtr.

**Composite arrangement
***Chord symbols reflect overall harmony.

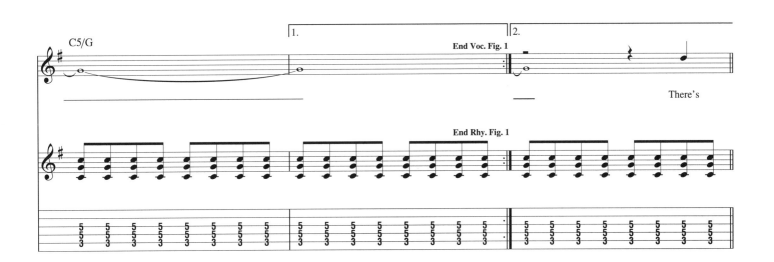

Intro

Bkgd. Voc.: w/ Voc. Fig. 1 (1 3/4 times)
Gtrs. 2 & 3: w/ Rhy. Fig. 1 (1 1/2 times)

so much more ___ that I want - ed ___ and ___ there's so much more ___ that I

need - ed and ___ time keeps mov - ing on and on ___ and on. ___

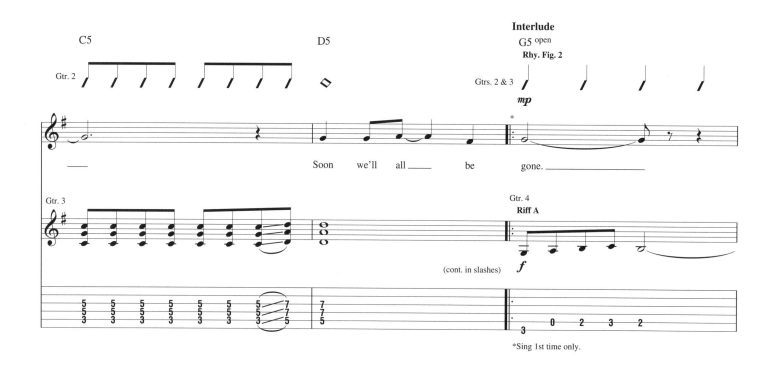

Soon we'll all ___ be gone. ___

(cont. in slashes)

*Sing 1st time only.

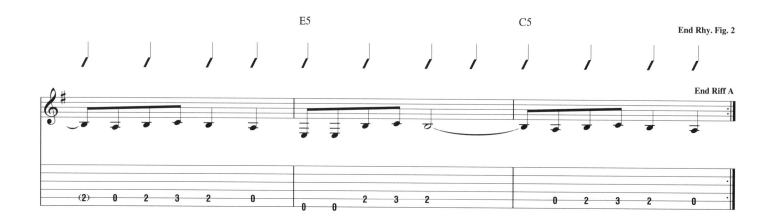

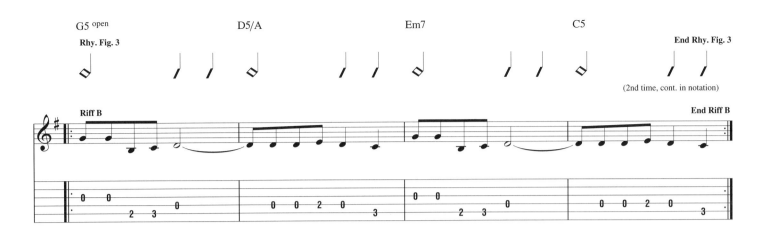

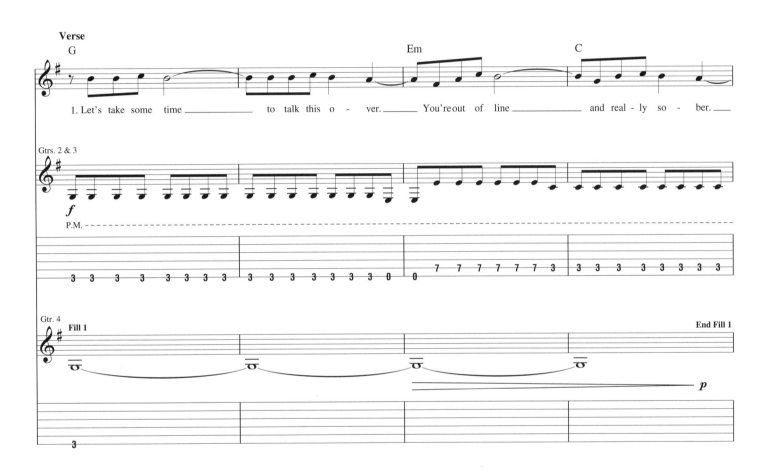

The Rock Show

Words and Music by Tom De Longe, Mark Hoppus and Travis Barker

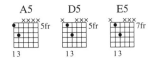

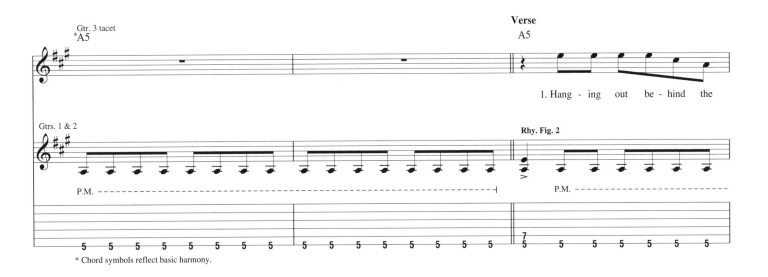

* Chord symbols reflect basic harmony.

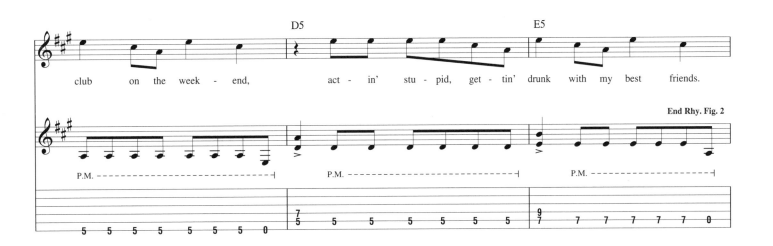

Gtrs. 1 & 2: w/ Rhy. Fig. 2

A5   D5

I could-n't wait for the sum-mer and the Warped Tour.   I re-mem-ber it's the

Interlude

Gtrs. 1 & 2: w/ Rhy. Fig. 1 (2 times)
Gtr. 3: w/ Riff A (2 times)

E5   A5   D5

first time that I saw her there.

E5   A5   D5   E5

Verse

A5   D5   E5

2. She's get - tin' kicked out of school 'cause she's fail - ing.   I'm kind - a ner - vous 'cause I think all her friends hate me.

Gtrs. 1 & 2

_pp_

A5   D5   E5

She's the one, she'll al - ways be there.   She took my hand and that made it I swear be - cause I

𝄋 **Chorus**

A5   F♯5   D5   A5   F♯5   D5

{1., 3. fell}
{2. Fell} in love with the girl at the rock show.   She said, "What?" And I told her that I did - n't know.

Gtrs. 1 & 2

_f_

Sev - en - teen with - out a pur - pose or dir - ec - tion. We don't owe an - y - one a fuck - in' ex - pla - na - tion.

⊕ Coda 1

Black and white pic - ture of her on my wall. I wait - ed

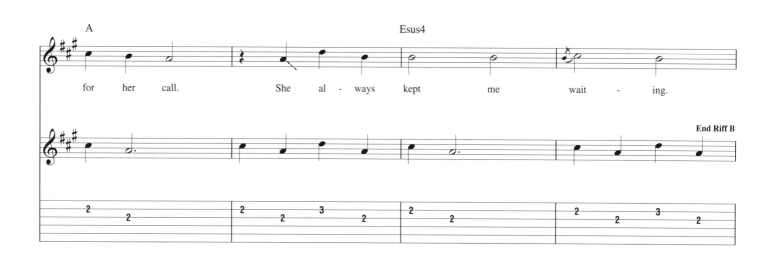

for her call. She al - ways kept me wait - ing.

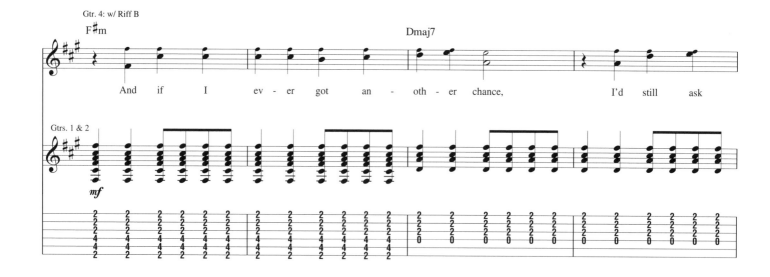

And if I ev - er got an - oth - er chance, I'd still ask

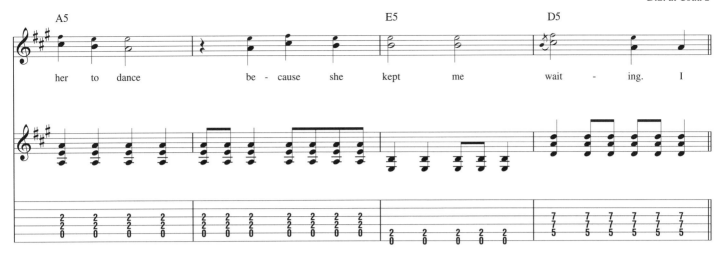

her to dance be - cause she kept me wait - ing. I

⊕ Coda 2

Outro

Gtrs. 1 & 2: w/ Rhy. Fig. 1 (till fade)
Gtr. 3: w/ Riff A (till fade)

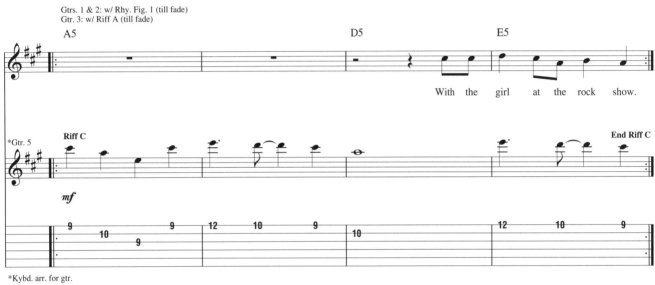

With the girl at the rock show.

*Kybd. arr. for gtr.

Gtr. 4: w/ Riff B (till fade)
Gtr. 5: w/ Riff C (till fade)

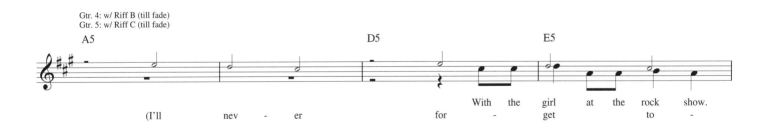

With the girl at the rock show.

(I'll nev - er for - get to -

Play 5 times and fade

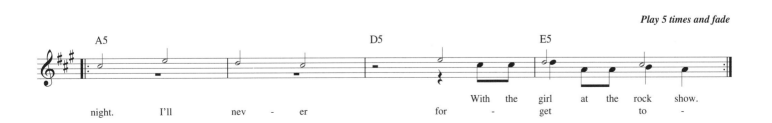

With the girl at the rock show.

night. I'll nev - er for - get to -

First Date

Words and Music by Tom De Longe, Mark Hoppus and Travis Barker

Stay Together for the Kids

Words and Music by Tom De Longe, Mark Hoppus and Travis Barker

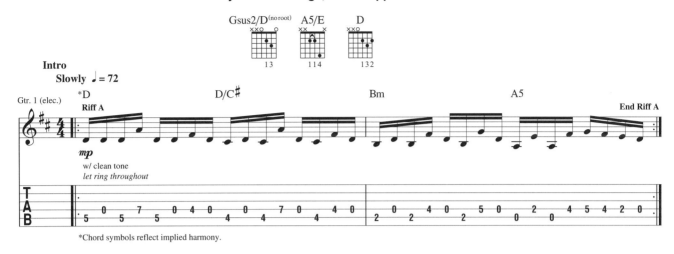

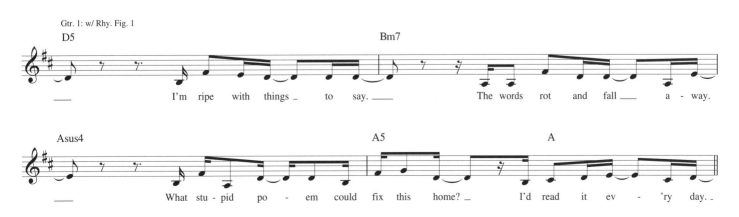

Interlude

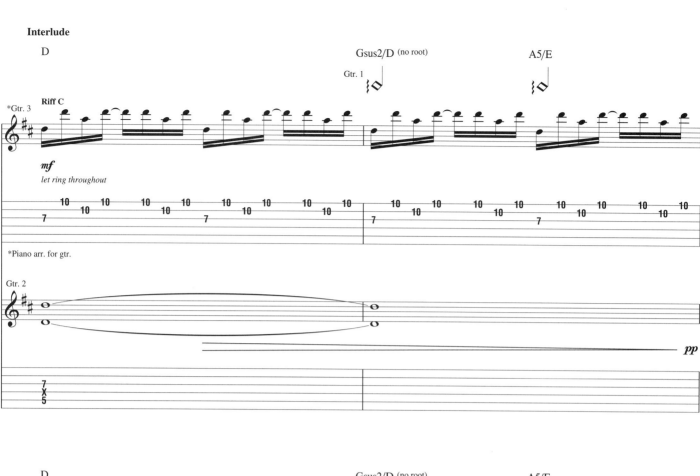

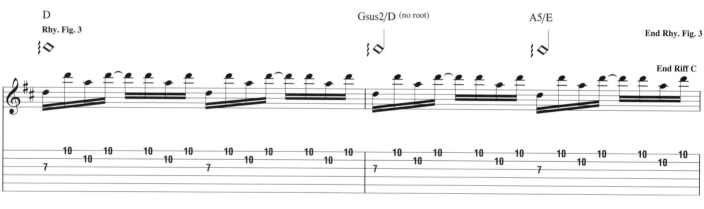

Chorus

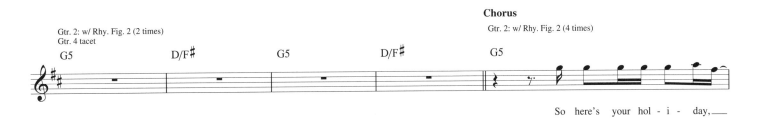

So here's your hol - i - day, ___

___ hope you en - joy it this time. You gave it all ___ a - way, ___ it was mine. ___

___ So when you're dead ___ and gone, ___ will you re - mem - ber this night? Twen - ty years ___ now lost, ___

Outro

Gtr. 2: w/ Rhy. Fig. 2 (till fade)

___ it's not right. It's not right, it's not right, ___ it's not right. ___

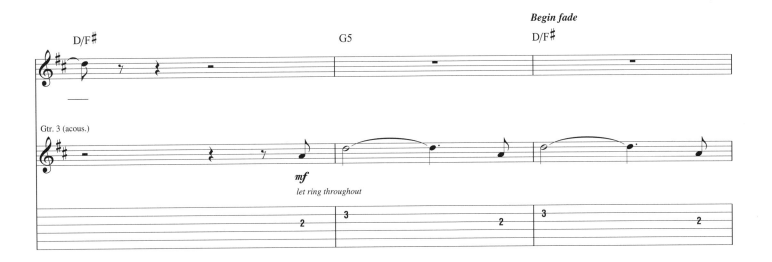

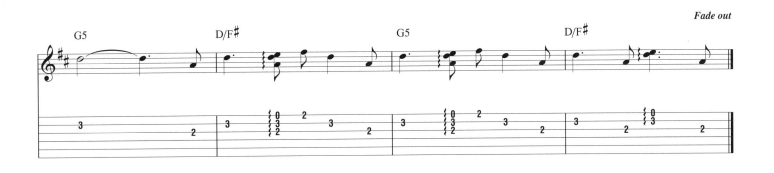

55

Feeling This

Words and Music by Travis Barker, Tom De Longe and Mark Hoppus

Verse

Gtr. 1: w/ Riff A
Gtrs. 2 & 3 tacet

E
(D)

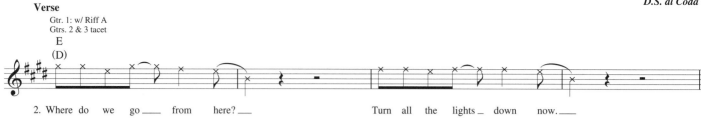

2. Where do we go ___ from here? ___   Turn all the lights ___ down now. ___

Coda

Gtr. 4 tacet

N.C.

Shouted: Fate   fell   short   this   time,   your   smile ___   fades   in   the   sum - mer.

Place   your   hand   in   mine,   I'll   leave   when   I   wan - na.

Bridge

E5

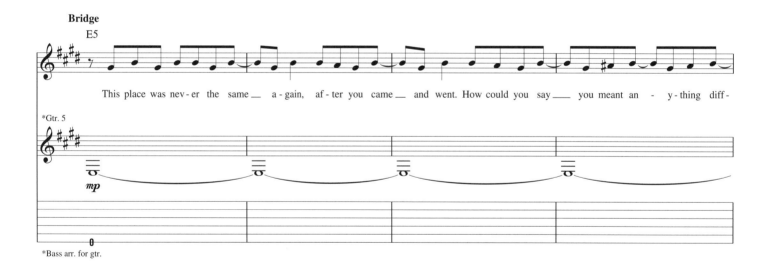

This place was nev - er the same ___ a - gain, af - ter you came ___ and went. How could you say ___ you meant an - y - thing diff-

*Gtr. 5

mp

*Bass arr. for gtr.

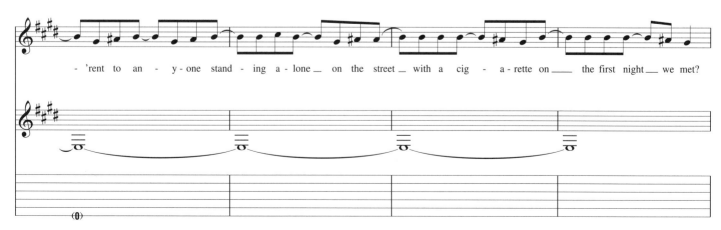

- 'rent to an - y - one stand - ing a - lone ___ on the street ___ with a cig - a - rette on ___ the first night ___ we met?

I Miss You

Words and Music by Travis Barker, Tom De Longe and Mark Hoppus

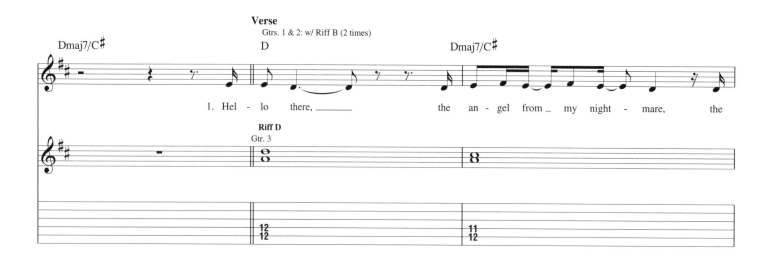

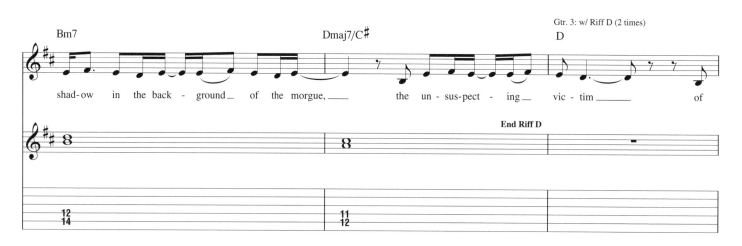

Bm7   Dmaj7/C#

in the night ___ we'll wish this nev - er ends, ___ we'll wish this nev - er ends, ___

End Riff E

Chorus

*** D5   Em7   F#m(add13)   A

Gtrs. 1 & 2   **Rhy. Fig. 1**

*Gtr. 4   **Riff F**

*Horns arr. for gtr.

Gtr. 5   **Riff F1

mf

**Acous. bass arr. for gtr.

    ***Chord symbols reflect implied harmony.

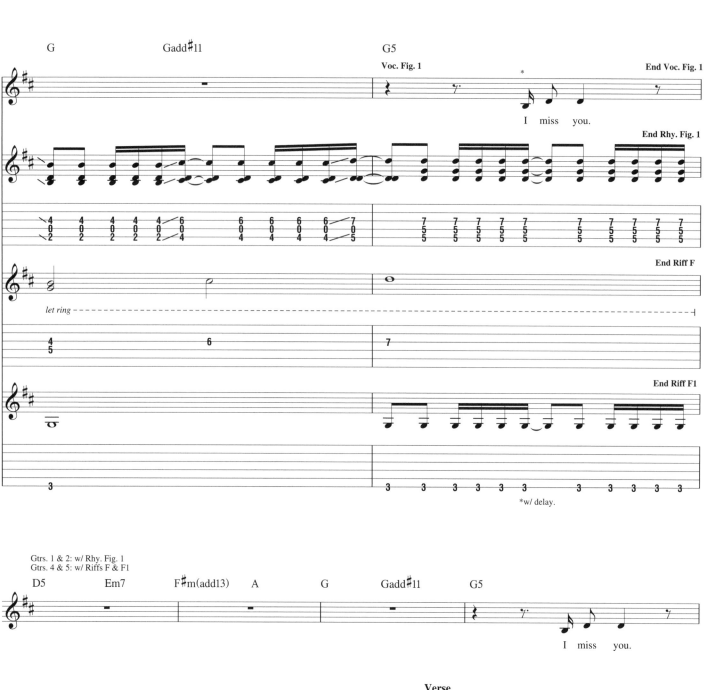

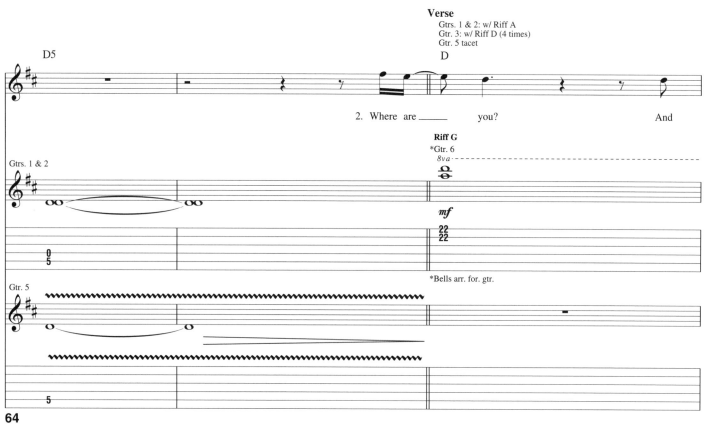

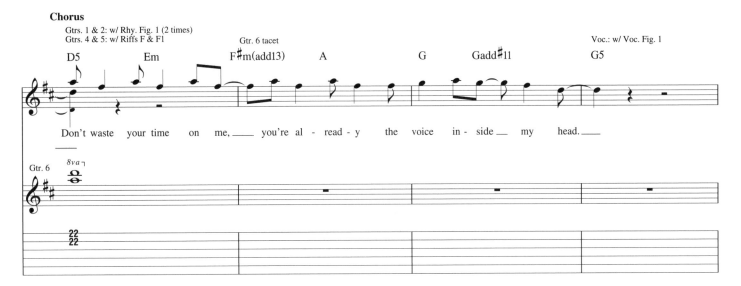

So waste your time on me, ____ you're al - read - y the voice in - side ____ my head. ____

Interlude

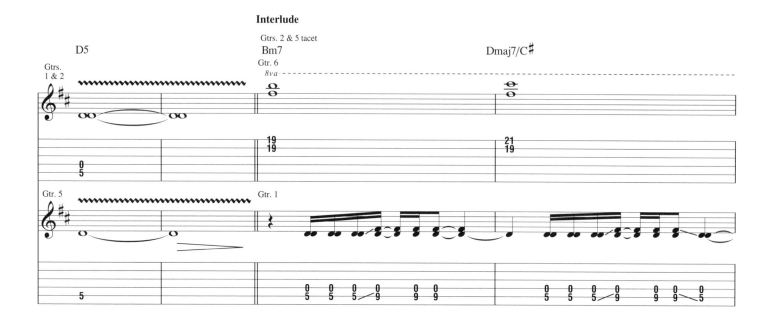

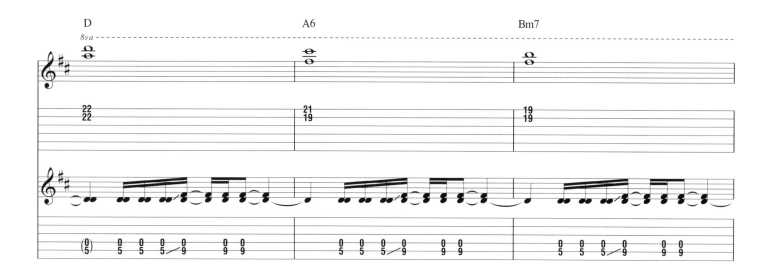

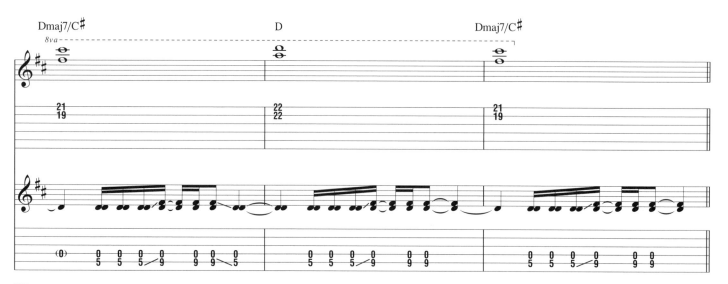

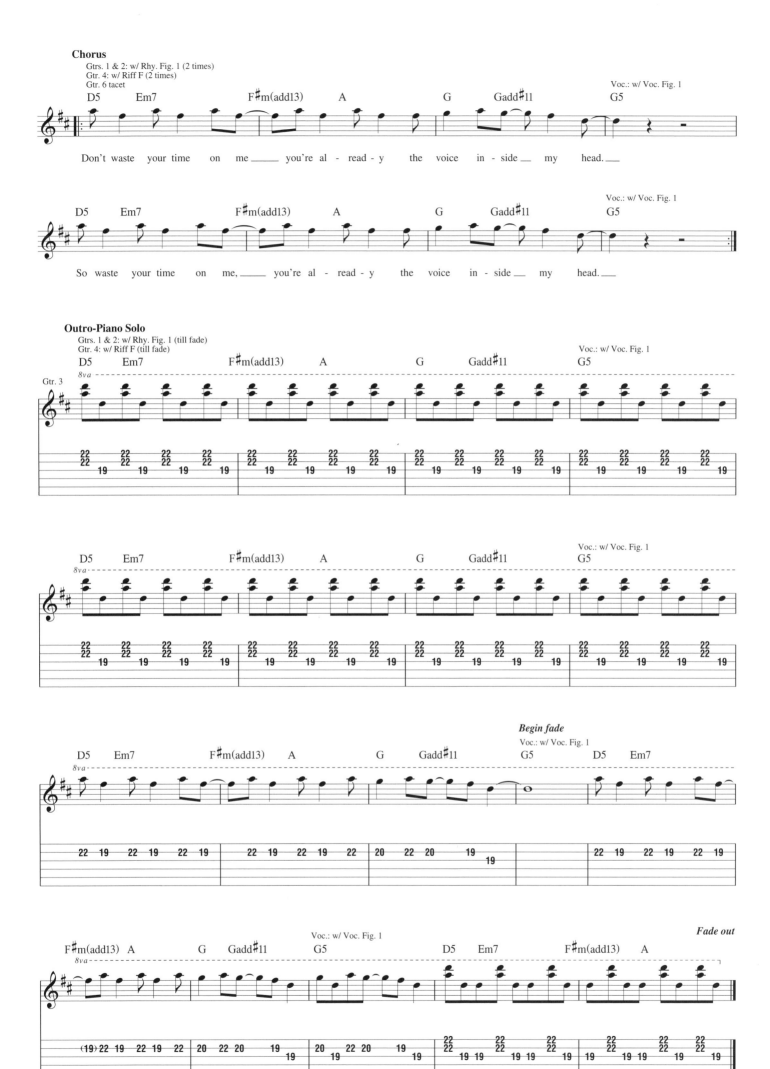

Down

Words and Music by Travis Barker, Tom De Longe and Mark Hoppus

Tune down 1 1/2 steps:
(low to high) C#-F#-B-E-G#-C#

Intro
Moderately ♩ = 94

* D5

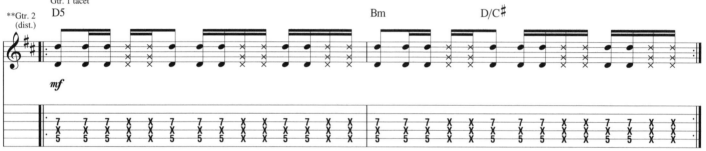

*Chord symbols reflect overall harmony.

**Doubled throughout

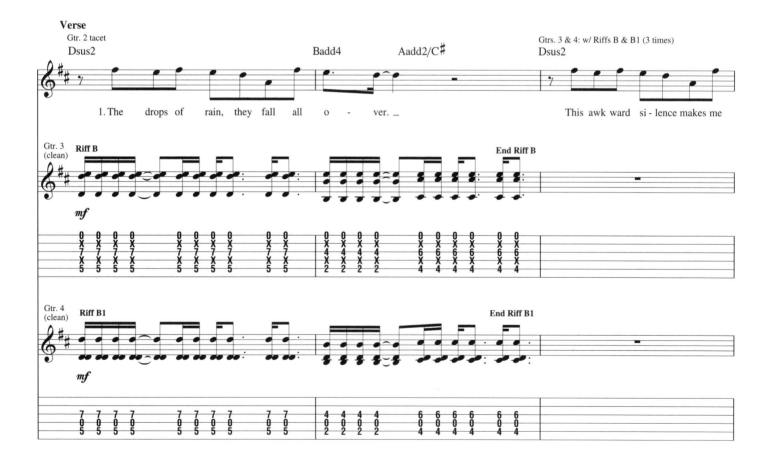

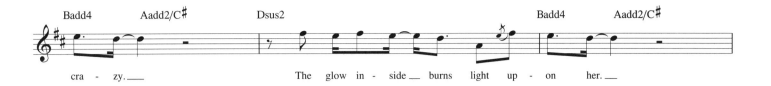

cra - zy.___ The glow in - side ___ burns light up - on - her.___

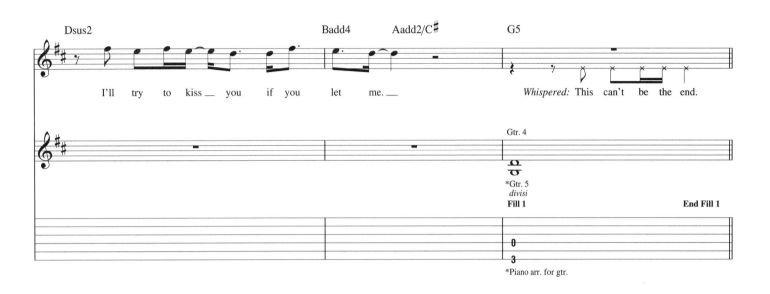

I'll try to kiss ___ you if you let me. ___ *Whispered:* This can't be the end.

*Gtr. 5
divisi

Fill 1   **End Fill 1**

*Piano arr. for gtr.

⅌ Pre-Chorus

Gtrs. 4 & 5 tacet

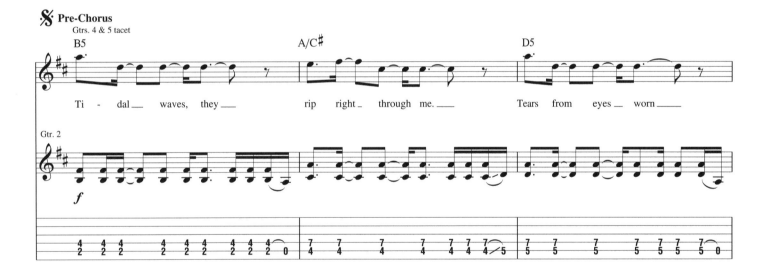

Ti - dal waves, they ___ rip right ___ through me. ___ Tears from eyes ___ worn ___

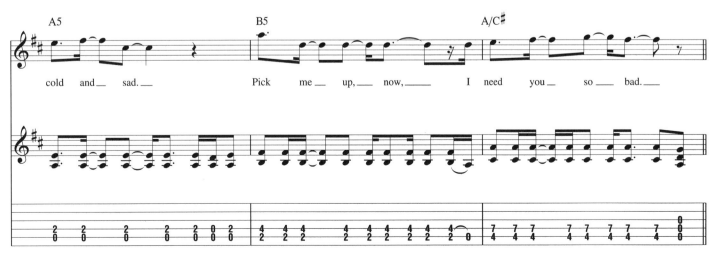

cold and ___ sad. ___ Pick me ___ up, ___ now, ___ I need you so ___ bad.

Chorus

Gtr. 2 tacet
2nd time, Gtr. 5: w/ Fill 2 (8 times)

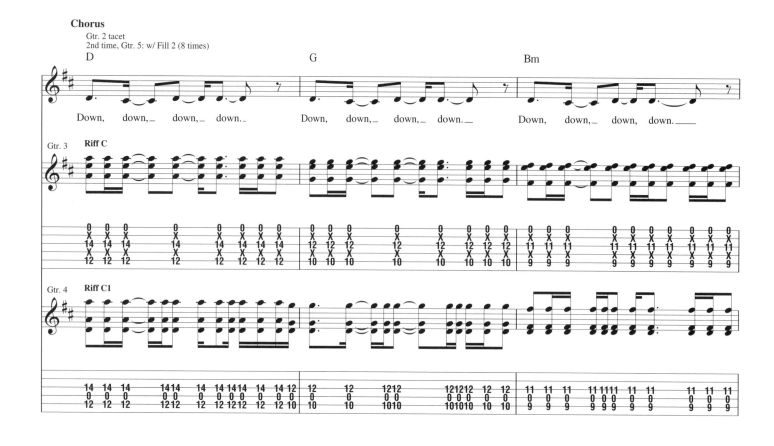

Down, down,_ down,_ down.   Down, down,_ down,_ down._   Down, down,_ down, down._____

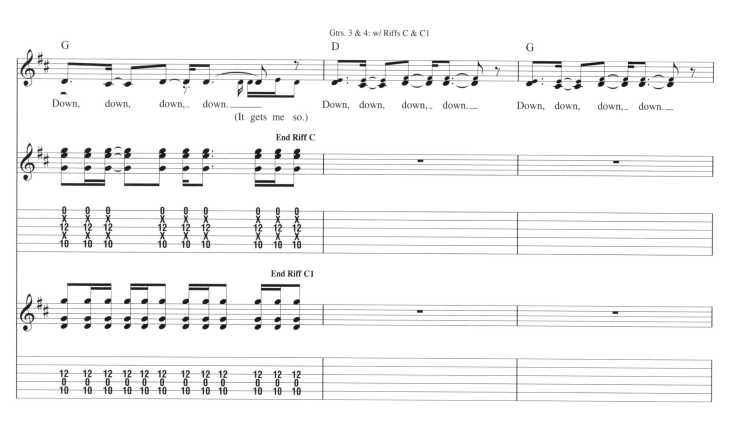

Gtrs. 3 & 4: w/ Riffs C & C1

Down, down, down,_ down.____   Down, down, down,_ down._   Down, down, down,_ down._

(It gets me so.)

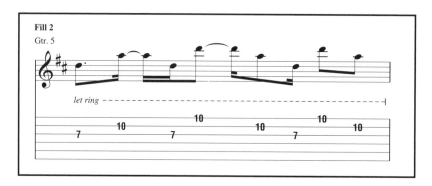

Fill 2
Gtr. 5

let ring -----------------------------------

70

Always

Words and Music by Travis Barker, Tom De Longe and Mark Hoppus

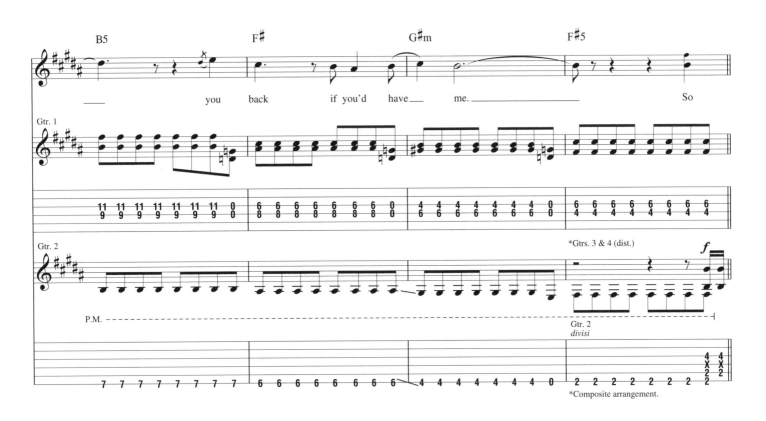

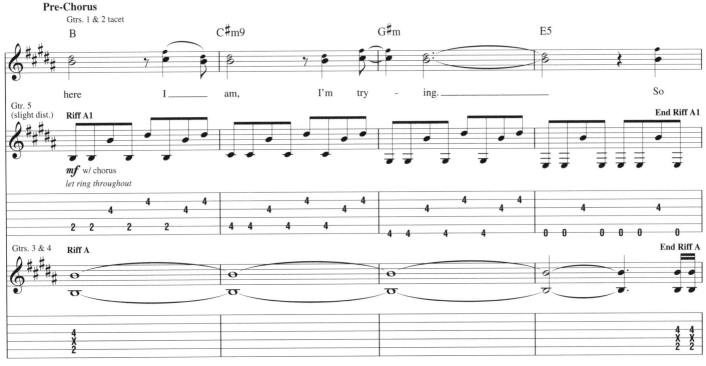

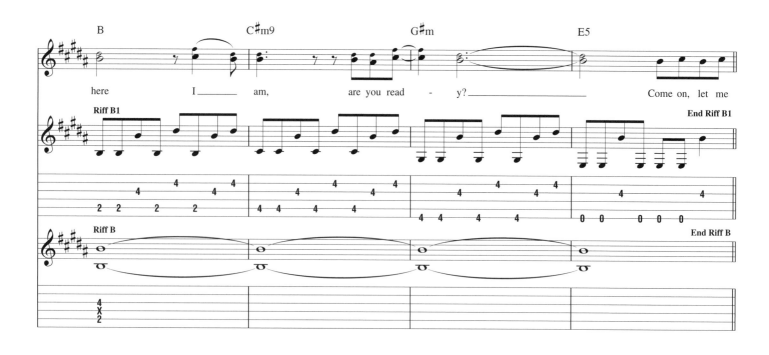

here I ____ am, are you read - y? _____ Come on, let me

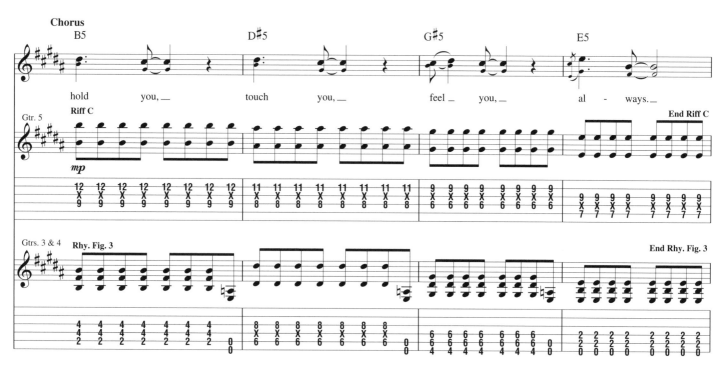

Chorus

hold you, __ touch you, __ feel _ you, _ al - ways. _

Kiss you, __ taste _ you, __ all night, _ al - ways. _

Interlude

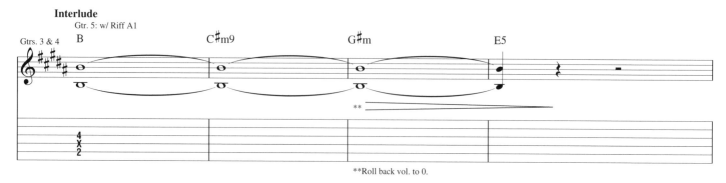

**Roll back vol. to 0.

Gtrs. 3 & 4: w/ Rhy. Fig. 3 (4 times)
Gtr. 5: w/ Riff C (4 times)

hold   you,   touch   you,   feel   you,   al - ways.

Kiss   you,   taste you,   all night,   al - ways.   Come on, let me

hold   you,   touch   you,   feel   you,   al - ways.

To Coda ⊕

Kiss   you,   taste you,   all night,   al - ways.

Interlude

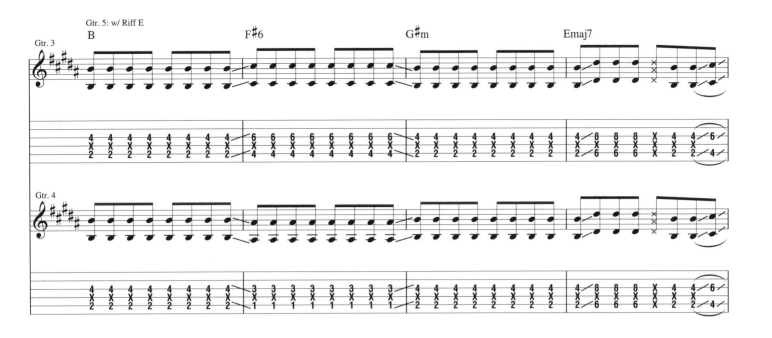

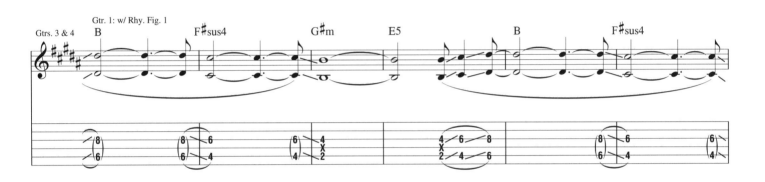

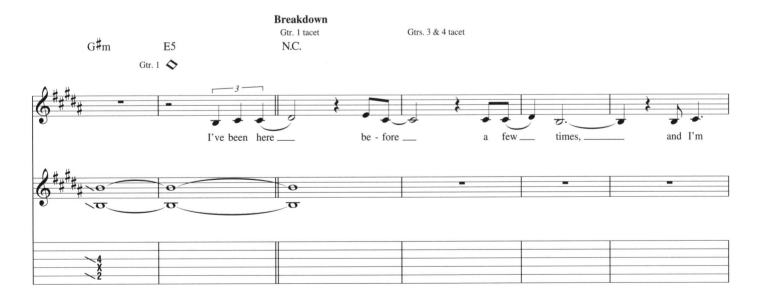

I've been here ___ be-fore ___ a few ___ times, ___ and I'm

quite a-ware ___ we're dy - ing. ___

Come on, let me

D.S. al Coda

⊕ Coda
Outro

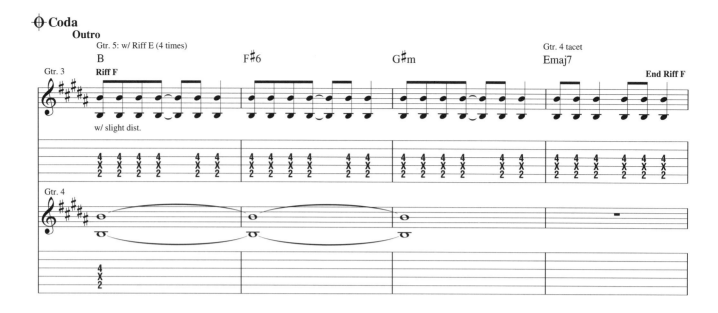

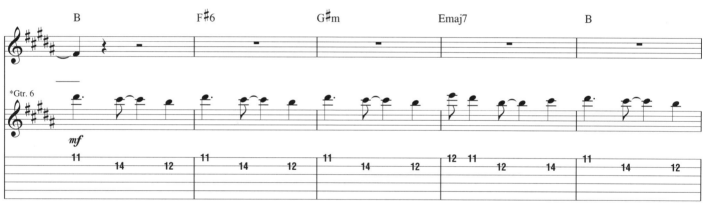

*Synth. arr. for gtr.

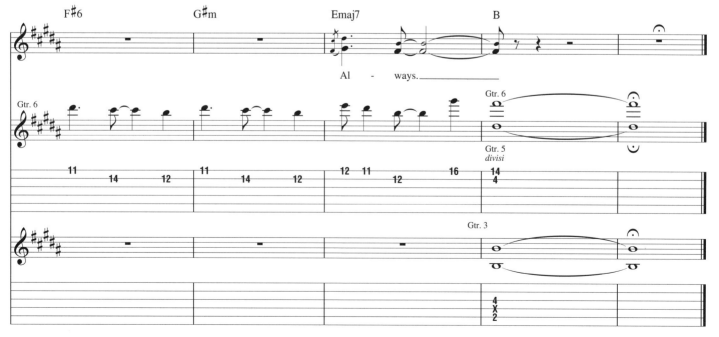

Not Now

Words and Music by Mark Hoppus, Tom De Longe and Travis Barker

Gtrs. 3, 4 & 5: Drop D tuning:
(low to high) D-A-D-G-B-E

Intro

Fast Rock ♩ = 216

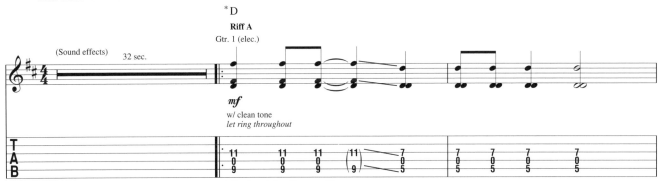

*Chord symbols reflect overall harmony.

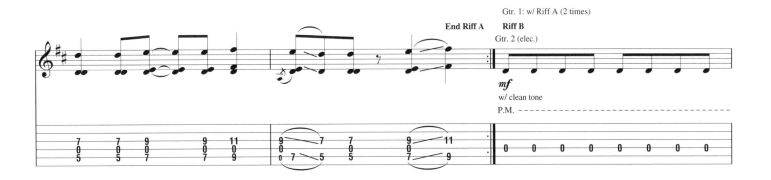

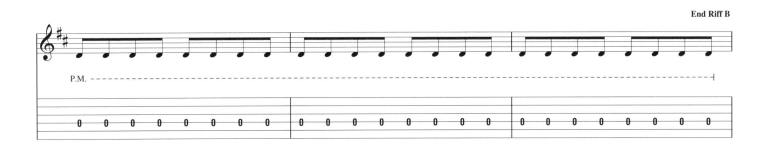

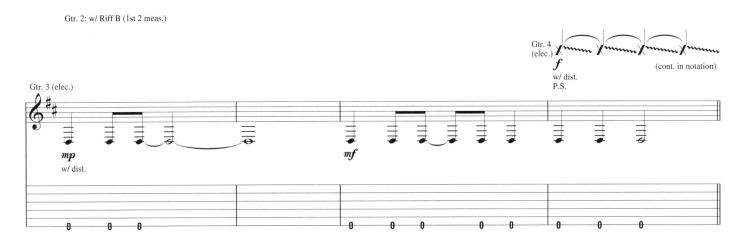

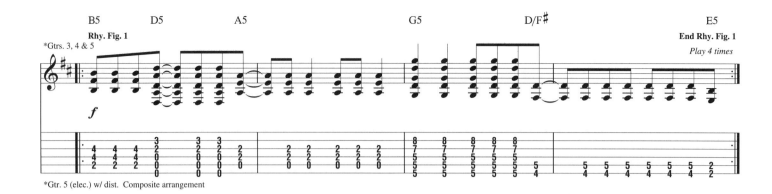

*Gtr. 5 (elec.) w/ dist. Composite arrangement

Verse

Gtrs. 3, 4 & 5 tacet

1. Come here, _____ please hold my hand_ for now. Help me. _____

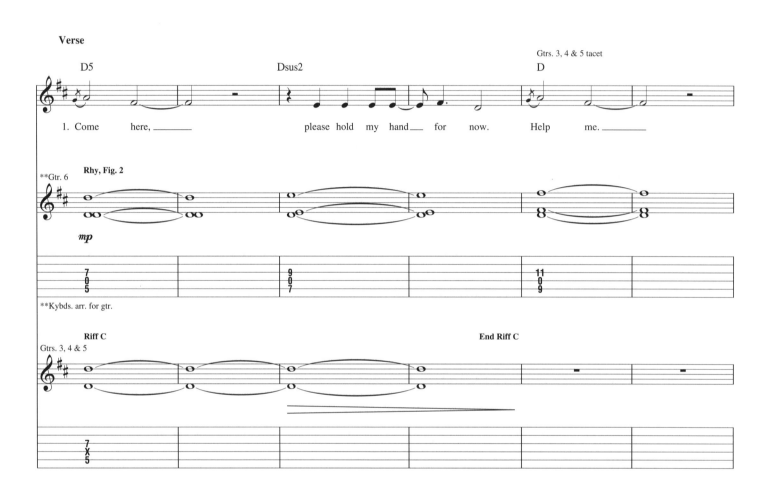

Rhy, Fig. 2

**Gtr. 6

**Kybds. arr. for gtr.

Riff C   **End Riff C**

Gtrs. 3, 4 & 5

I'm scared, please show me how_ to fight this. _____ God has a mas - ter plan_ and

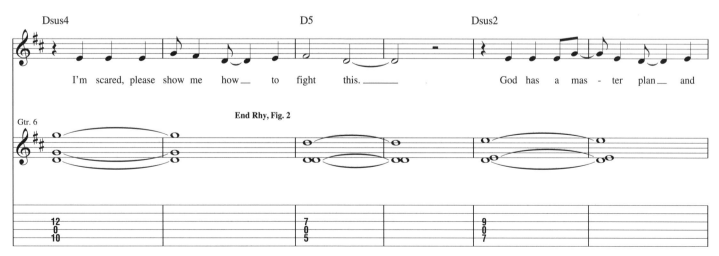

End Rhy, Fig. 2

Gtr. 6

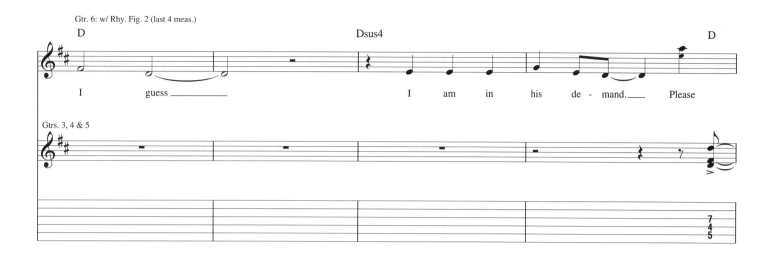

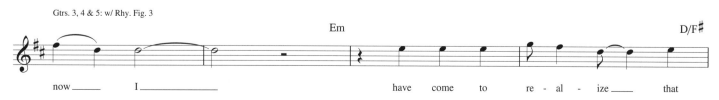

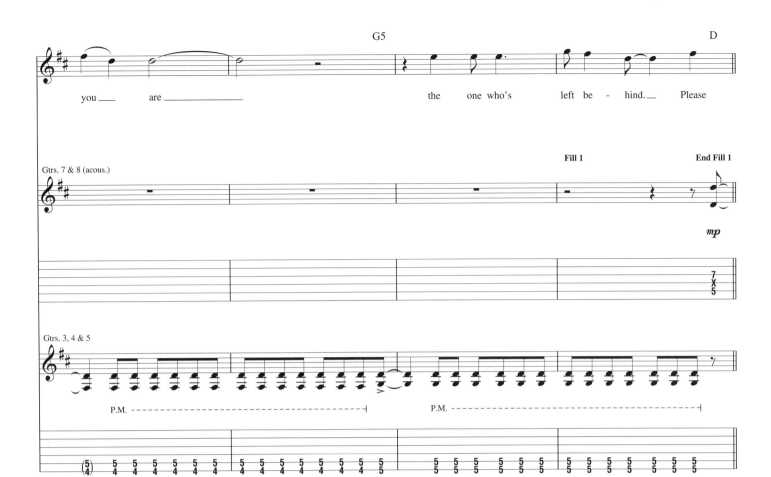

Chorus

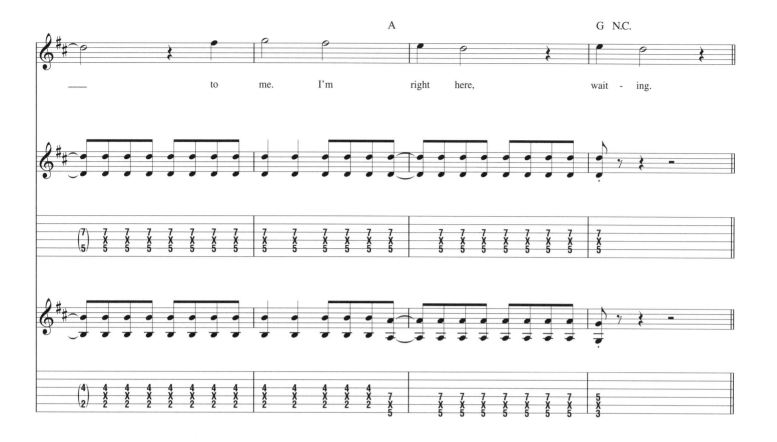

to me. I'm right here, wait-ing.

Interlude

Gtrs. 3, 4 & 5: w/ Rhy. Fig. 1 (2 times)
Gtrs. 7 & 8 tacet

| B5 | D5/A | A5 | G5 | D/F# | E5 |

Verse

Gtrs. 3, 4 & 5: w/ Riff C
Gtr. 6: w/ Rhy. Fig. 2 (2 times)

D5   Dsus2   D

2. I see _____ a light, it feels good.__ And I'll come _____
   (I see._____   And I'll come. ____

Gtr. 2: w/ Riff B (2 times)

Dsus4   D5   Dsus2

back soon just like you would.__ It's use-less, _____ my name has
_____   It's use-less. _____

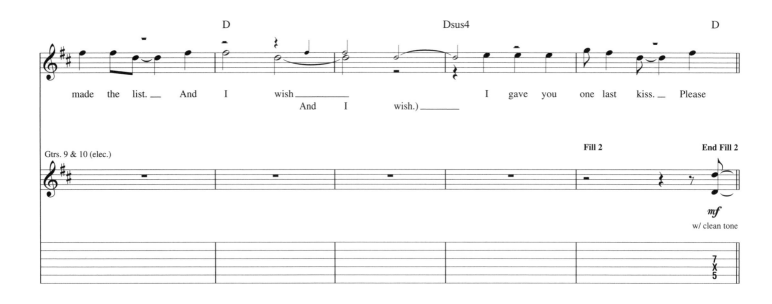

made the list. ___ And I wish _____ (And I wish.) _____ I gave you one last kiss. ___ Please

Gtrs. 9 & 10 (elec.)

Fill 2   End Fill 2

mf
w/ clean tone

Chorus
Gtr. 9: w/ Riff D1
Gtr. 10: w/ Riff D

stay   un - til   I'm   gone. ___   I'm   here,   hold   on ___

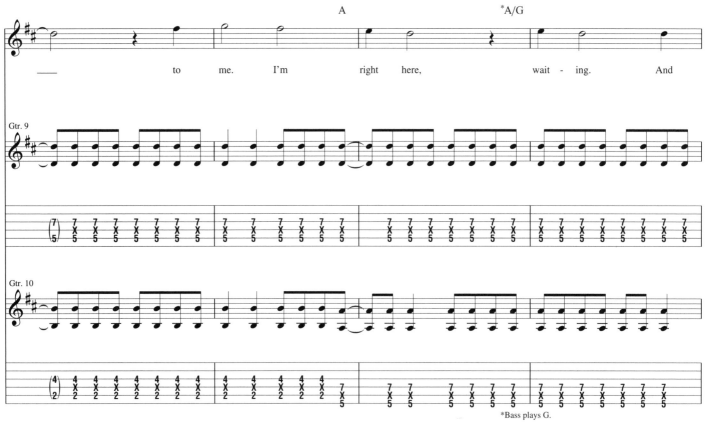

___   to   me.   I'm   right   here,   wait - ing.   And

Gtr. 9

Gtr. 10

*Bass plays G.

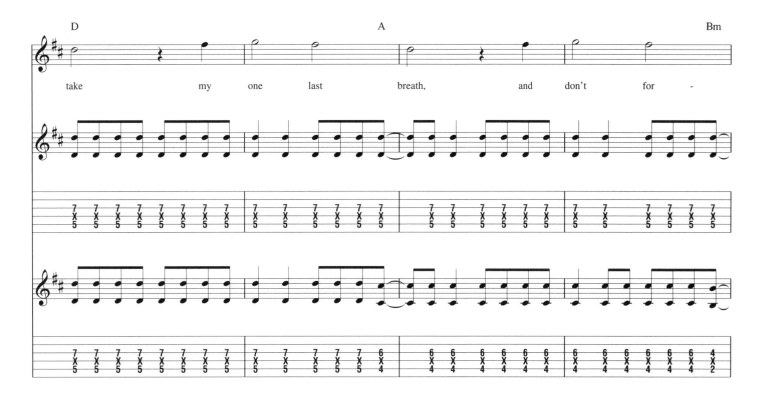

take my one last breath, and don't for -

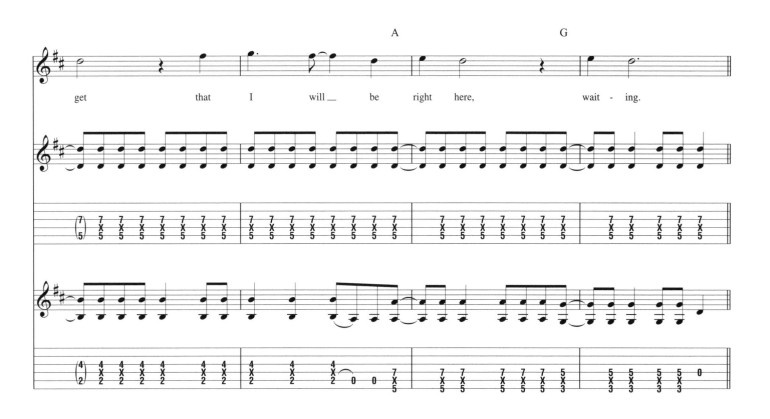

get that I will __ be right here, wait - ing.

Interlude

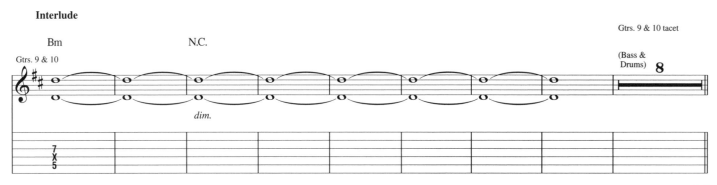

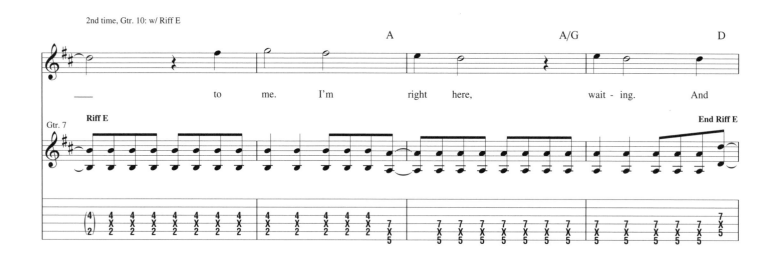

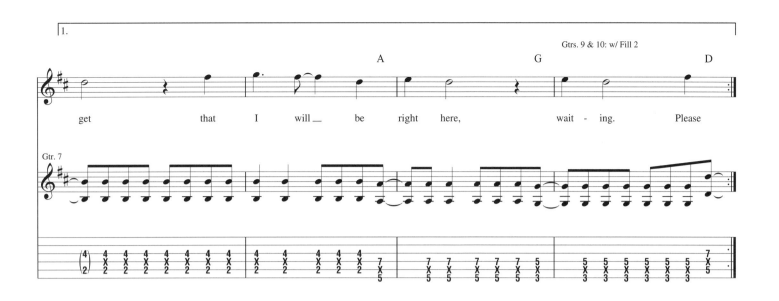

1.

Gtrs. 9 & 10: w/ Fill 2

A   G   D

get   that I will __ be   right here,   wait - ing.   Please

Gtr. 7

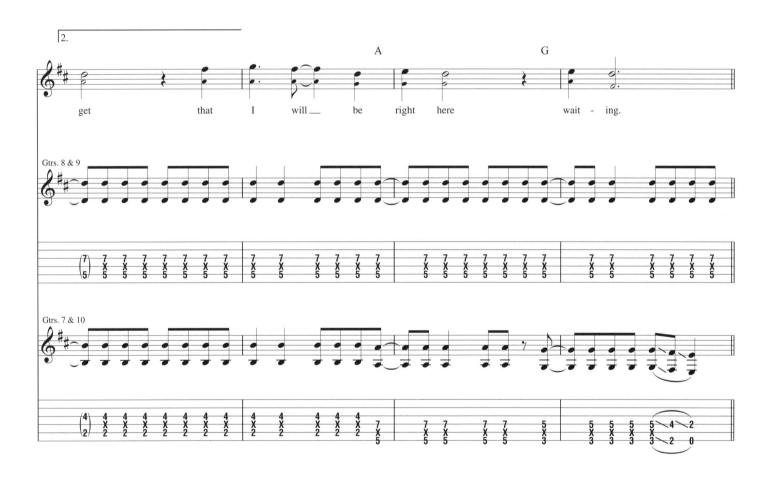

2.

A   G

get   that I will __ be   right here   wait - ing.

Gtrs. 8 & 9

Gtrs. 7 & 10

Outro

Gtrs. 3, 4 & 5: w/ Rhy. Fig. 1 (4 times)
Gtrs. 7–10 tacet

B5   D5   A5   G5   D/F#   E5 B5 D5 A5

Play 4 times

Gtrs. 3, 4 & 5

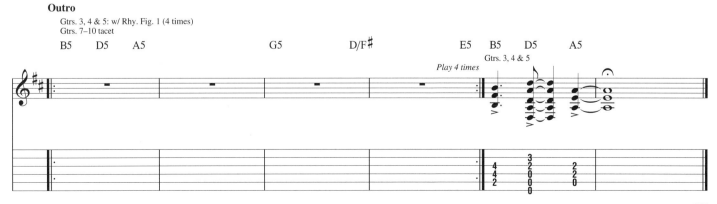

Another Girl Another Planet

Words and Music by Peter Perrett

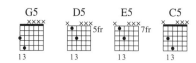

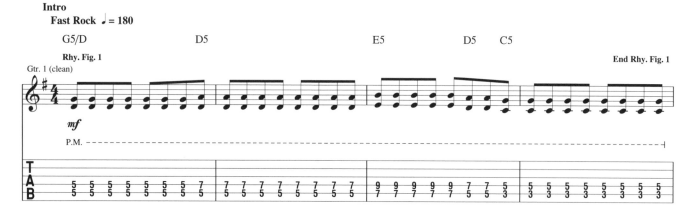

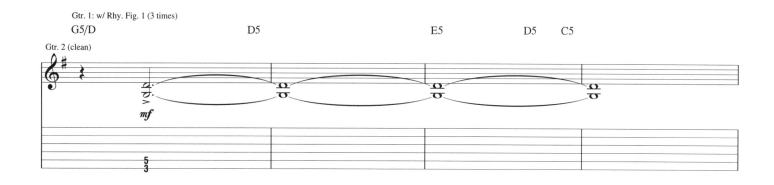

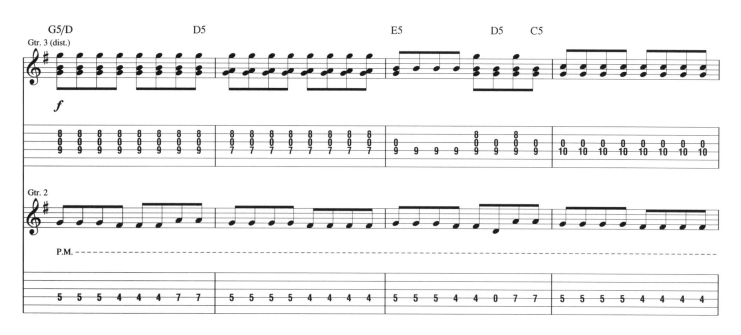

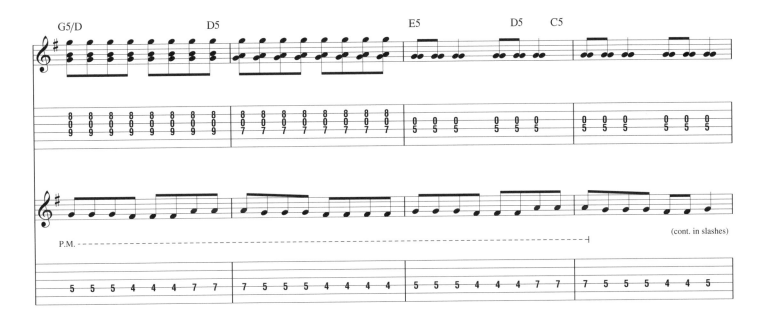

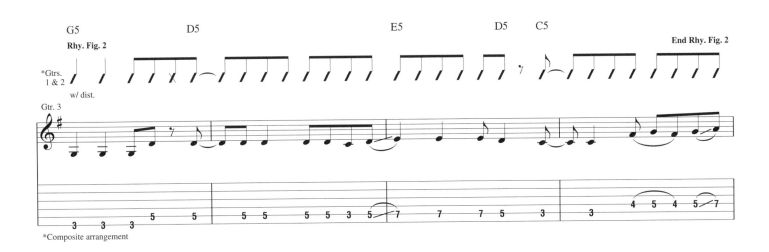

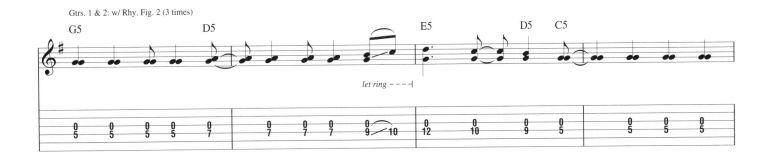

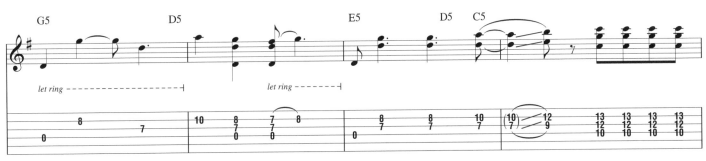

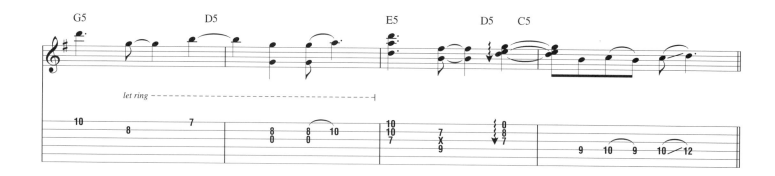

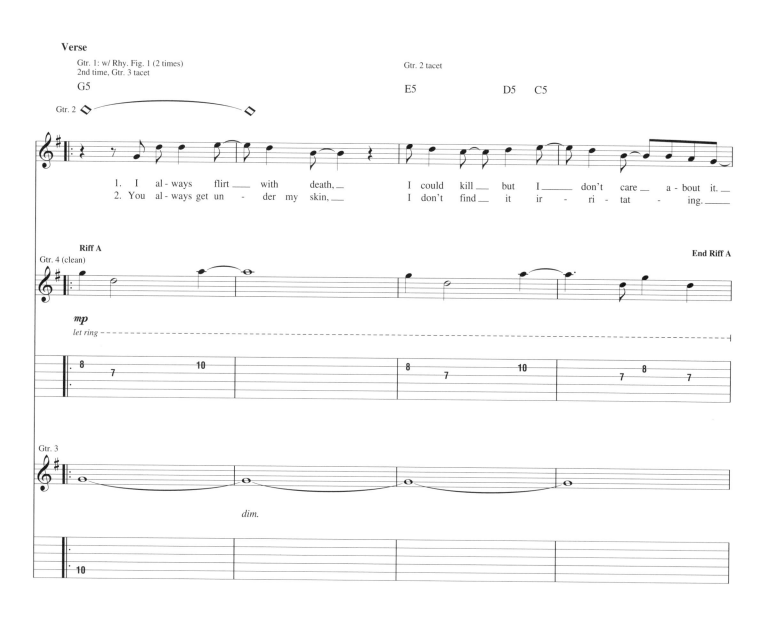

Chorus

I think I'm on an-oth-er world with you, with you.

I'm on an-oth-er plan-et with you, with you.

(An-oth-er girl, an-oth-er plan-et. An-oth-er girl, an-oth-er plan-et.)

Interlude

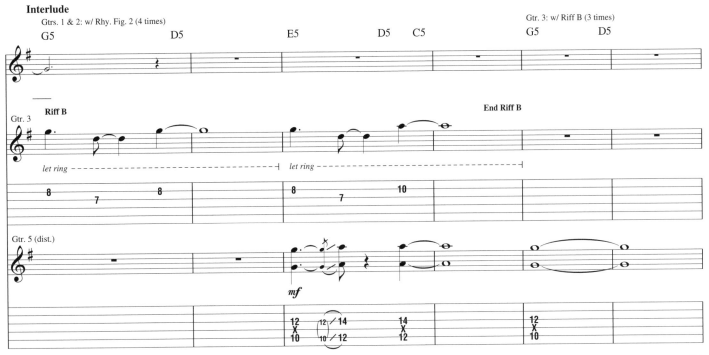

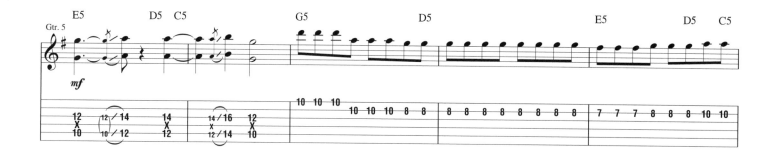

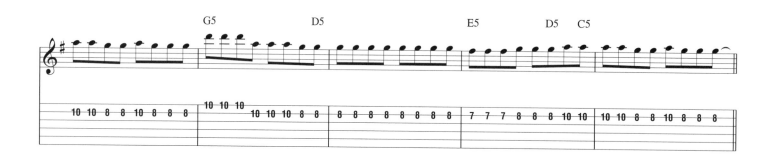

Verse

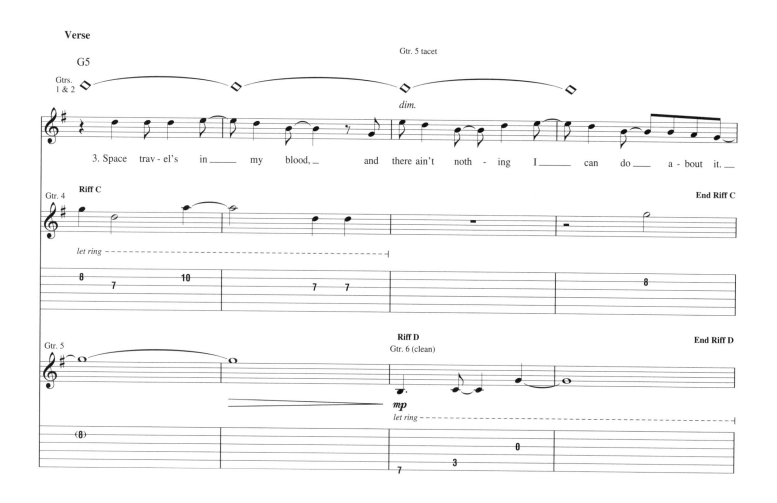

3. Space trav-el's in ____ my blood, ___ and there ain't noth - ing I ____ can do ___ a-bout it.

____ Long jour-neys wear ___ me out. ___ Oh, God, you ___ know we ___ won't live ___ with-out it. ___

*Chord symbols reflect overall harmony.

Chorus

Gtrs. 1 & 2: w/ Rhy. Fig. 3 (2 times)
2nd time, Gtr. 4: w/ Riff A (2 times)

*2nd time, voc. tacet on beat 1.

I think I'm on an-oth-er world with you, with you.

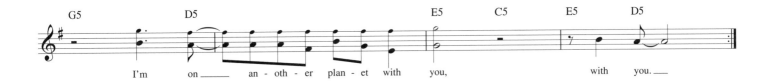

I'm on an-oth-er plan-et with you, with you.

Outro

Gtrs. 1 & 2: w/ Rhy. Fig. 2 (1 1/2 times)

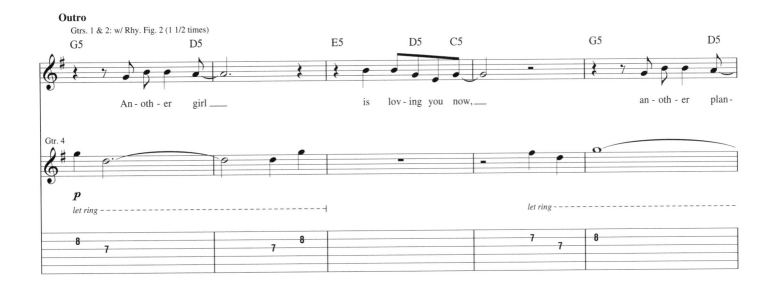

An-oth-er girl is lov-ing you now, an-oth-er plan-

Gtr. 4

p

let ring ---------------------------- let ring -----------------------------

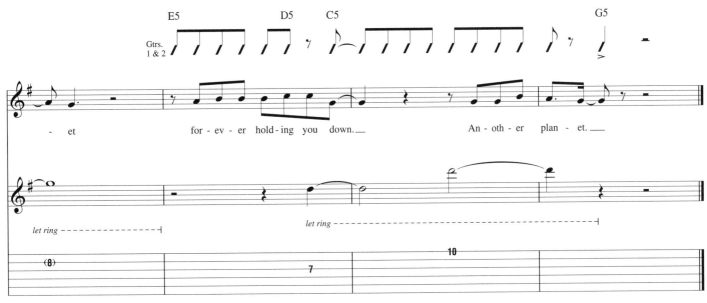

-et for-ev-er hold-ing you down. An-oth-er plan-et.

let ring --------------------- let ring ---------------------------

Guitar Notation Legend

Guitar Music can be notated three different ways: on a *musical staff*, in *tablature*, and in *rhythm slashes*.

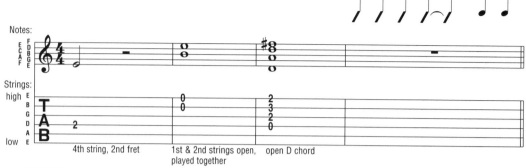

RHYTHM SLASHES are written above the staff. Strum chords in the rhythm indicated. Use the chord diagrams found at the top of the first page of the transcription for the appropriate chord voicings. Round noteheads indicate single notes.

THE MUSICAL STAFF shows pitches and rhythms and is divided by bar lines into measures. Pitches are named after the first seven letters of the alphabet.

TABLATURE graphically represents the guitar fingerboard. Each horizontal line represents a string, and each number represents a fret.

4th string, 2nd fret

1st & 2nd strings open, played together

open D chord

HALF-STEP BEND: Strike the note and bend up 1/2 step.

WHOLE-STEP BEND: Strike the note and bend up one step.

GRACE NOTE BEND: Strike the note and immediately bend up as indicated.

SLIGHT (MICROTONE) BEND: Strike the note and bend up 1/4 step.

BEND AND RELEASE: Strike the note and bend up as indicated, then release back to the original note. Only the first note is struck.

PRE-BEND: Bend the note as indicated, then strike it.

VIBRATO: The string is vibrated by rapidly bending and releasing the note with the fretting hand.

WIDE VIBRATO: The pitch is varied to a greater degree by vibrating with the fretting hand.

HAMMER-ON: Strike the first (lower) note with one finger, then sound the higher note (on the same string) with another finger by fretting it without picking.

PULL-OFF: Place both fingers on the notes to be sounded. Strike the first note and without picking, pull the finger off to sound the second (lower) note.

LEGATO SLIDE: Strike the first note and then slide the same fret-hand finger up or down to the second note. The second note is not struck.

SHIFT SLIDE: Same as legato slide, except the second note is struck.

TRILL: Very rapidly alternate between the notes indicated by continuously hammering on and pulling off.

TAPPING: Hammer ("tap") the fret indicated with the pick-hand index or middle finger and pull off to the note fretted by the fret hand.

NATURAL HARMONIC: Strike the note while the fret-hand lightly touches the string directly over the fret indicated.

PINCH HARMONIC: The note is fretted normally and a harmonic is produced by adding the edge of the thumb or the tip of the index finger of the pick hand to the normal pick attack.

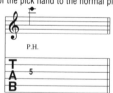

PICK SCRAPE: The edge of the pick is rubbed down (or up) the string, producing a scratchy sound.

MUFFLED STRINGS: A percussive sound is produced by laying the fret hand across the string(s) without depressing, and striking them with the pick hand.

PALM MUTING: The note is partially muted by the pick hand lightly touching the string(s) just before the bridge.

RAKE: Drag the pick across the strings indicated with a single motion.

TREMOLO PICKING: The note is picked as rapidly and continuously as possible.

VIBRATO BAR DIVE AND RETURN: The pitch of the note or chord is dropped a specified number of steps (in rhythm) then returned to the original pitch.

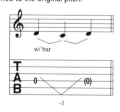

VIBRATO BAR SCOOP: Depress the bar just before striking the note, then quickly release the bar.

VIBRATO BAR DIP: Strike the note and then immediately drop a specified number of steps, then release back to the original pitch.

HAL•LEONARD GUITAR PLAY•ALONG®

This series will help you play your favorite songs quickly and easily. Just follow the tab and listen to the CD to hear how the guitar should sound, and then play along using the separate backing tracks. Mac or PC users can also slow down the tempo without changing pitch by using the CD in their computer. The melody and lyrics are included in the book so that you can sing or simply follow along.

INCLUDES TAB

VOL. 1 – ROCK GUITAR
00699570 / $14.95
Day Tripper • Message in a Bottle • Refugee • Shattered • Sunshine of Your Love • Takin' Care of Business • Tush • Walk This Way.

VOL. 2 – ACOUSTIC
00699569 / $14.95
Angie • Behind Blue Eyes • Best of My Love • Blackbird • Dust in the Wind • Layla • Night Moves • Yesterday.

VOL. 3 – HARD ROCK
00699573 / $14.95
Crazy Train • Iron Man • Living After Midnight • Rock You like a Hurricane • Round and Round • Smoke on the Water • Sweet Child O' Mine • You Really Got Me.

VOL. 4 – POP/ROCK
00699571 / $14.95
Breakdown • Crazy Little Thing Called Love • Hit Me with Your Best Shot • I Want You to Want Me • Lights • R.O.C.K. in the U.S.A. • Summer of '69 • What I Like About You.

VOL. 5 – MODERN ROCK
00699574 / $14.95
Aerials • Alive • Bother • Chop Suey! • Control • Last Resort • Take a Look Around (Theme from *M:I-2*) • Wish You Were Here.

VOL. 6 – '90S ROCK
00699572 / $14.95
Are You Gonna Go My Way • Come Out and Play • I'll Stick Around • Know Your Enemy • Man in the Box • Outshined • Smells Like Teen Spirit • Under the Bridge.

VOL. 7 – BLUES GUITAR
00699575 / $14.95
All Your Love (I Miss Loving) • Born Under a Bad Sign • Hide Away • I'm Tore Down • I'm Your Hoochie Coochie Man • Pride and Joy • Sweet Home Chicago • The Thrill Is Gone.

VOL. 8 – ROCK
00699585 / $14.95
All Right Now • Black Magic Woman • Get Back • Hey Joe • Layla • Love Me Two Times • Won't Get Fooled Again • You Really Got Me.

VOL. 9 – PUNK ROCK
00699576 / $14.95
All the Small Things • Fat Lip • Flavor of the Weak • I Feel So • Lifestyles of the Rich and Famous• Say It Ain't So • Self Esteem • (So) Tired of Waiting for You.

VOL. 10 – ACOUSTIC
00699586 / $14.95
Here Comes the Sun • Landslide • The Magic Bus • Norwegian Wood (This Bird Has Flown) • Pink Houses • Space Oddity • Tangled Up in Blue • Tears in Heaven.

VOL. 11 – EARLY ROCK
00699579 / $14.95
Fun, Fun, Fun • Hound Dog • Louie, Louie • No Particular Place to Go • Oh, Pretty Woman • Rock Around the Clock • Under the Boardwalk • Wild Thing.

VOL. 12 – POP/ROCK
00699587 / $14.95
867-5309/Jenny • Every Breath You Take • Money for Nothing • Rebel, Rebel • Run to You • Ticket to Ride • Wonderful Tonight • You Give Love a Bad Name.

VOL. 13 – FOLK ROCK
00699581 / $14.95
Annie's Song • Leaving on a Jet Plane • Suite: Judy Blue Eyes • This Land Is Your Land • Time in a Bottle • Turn! Turn! Turn! • You've Got a Friend • You've Got to Hide Your Love Away.

VOL. 14 – BLUES ROCK
00699582 / $14.95
Blue on Black • Crossfire • Cross Road Blues (Crossroads) • The House Is Rockin' • La Grange • Move It on Over • Roadhouse Blues • Statesboro Blues.

VOL. 15 – R&B
00699583 / $14.95
Ain't Too Proud to Beg • Brick House • Get Ready • I Can't Help Myself • I Got You (I Feel Good) • I Heard It Through the Grapevine • My Girl • Shining Star.

VOL. 16 – JAZZ
00699584 / $14.95
All Blues • Bluesette • Footprints • How Insensitive • Misty • Satin Doll • Stella by Starlight • Tenor Madness.

VOL. 17 – COUNTRY
00699588 / $14.95
Amie • Boot Scootin' Boogie • Chattahoochee • Folsom Prison Blues • Friends in Low Places • Forever and Ever, Amen • T-R-O-U-B-L-E • Workin' Man Blues.

VOL. 18 – ACOUSTIC ROCK
00699577 / $14.95
About a Girl • Breaking the Girl • Drive • Iris • More Than Words • Patience • Silent Lucidity • 3 AM.

VOL. 19 – SOUL
00699578 / $14.95
Get Up (I Feel Like Being) a Sex Machine • Green Onions • In the Midnight Hour • Knock on Wood • Mustang Sally • Respect • (Sittin' On) the Dock of the Bay • Soul Man.

VOL. 20 – ROCKABILLY
00699580 / $14.95
Be-Bop-A-Lula • Blue Suede Shoes • Hello Mary Lou • Little Sister • Mystery Train • Rock This Town • Stray Cat Strut • That'll Be the Day.

VOL. 21 – YULETIDE
00699602 / $14.95
Angels We Have Heard on High • Away in a Manger • Deck the Hall • The First Noel • Go, Tell It on the Mountain • Jingle Bells • Joy to the World • O Little Town of Bethlehem.

VOL. 22 – CHRISTMAS
00699600 / $14.95
The Christmas Song • Frosty the Snow Man • Happy Xmas • Here Comes Santa Claus • Jingle-Bell Rock • Merry Christmas, Darling • Rudolph the Red-Nosed Reindeer • Silver Bells.

VOL. 23 – SURF
00699635 / $14.95
Let's Go Trippin' • Out of Limits • Penetration • Pipeline • Surf City • Surfin' U.S.A. • Walk Don't Run • The Wedge.

VOL. 24 – ERIC CLAPTON
00699649 / $14.95
Badge • Bell Bottom Blues • Change the World • Cocaine • Key to the Highway • Lay Down Sally • White Room • Wonderful Tonight.

VOL. 25 – LENNON & McCARTNEY
00699642 / $14.95
Back in the U.S.S.R. • Drive My Car • Get Back • A Hard Day's Night • I Feel Fine • Paperback Writer • Revolution • Ticket to Ride.

VOL. 26 – ELVIS PRESLEY
00699643 / $14.95
All Shook Up • Blue Suede Shoes • Don't Be Cruel • Heartbreak Hotel • Hound Dog • Jailhouse Rock • Little Sister • Mystery Train.

VOL. 27 – DAVID LEE ROTH
00699645 / $14.95
Ain't Talkin' 'Bout Love • Dance the Night Away • Hot for Teacher • Just Like Paradise • A Lil' Ain't Enough • Runnin' with the Devil • Unchained • Yankee Rose.

VOL. 28 – GREG KOCH
00699646 / $14.95
Chief's Blues • Death of a Bassman • Dylan the Villain • The Grip • Holy Grail • Spank It • Tonus Diabolicus • Zoiks.

VOL. 29 – BOB SEGER
00699647 / $14.95
Against the Wind • Betty Lou's Gettin' Out Tonight • Hollywood Nights • Mainstreet • Night Moves • Old Time Rock & Roll • Rock and Roll Never Forgets • Still the Same.

VOL. 30 – KISS
00699644 / $14.95
Cold Gin • Detroit Rock City • Deuce • Firehouse • Heaven's on Fire • Love Gun • Rock and Roll All Nite • Shock Me.

VOL. 31 – CHRISTMAS HITS
00699652 / $14.95
Blue Christmas • Do You Hear What I Hear • Happy Holiday • I Saw Mommy Kissing Santa Claus • I'll Be Home for Christmas • Let It Snow! Let It Snow! Let It Snow! • Little Saint Nick • Snowfall.

VOL. 32 – THE OFFSPRING
00699653 / $14.95
Bad Habit • Come Out and Play • Gone Away • Gotta Get Away • Hit That • The Kids Aren't Alright • Pretty Fly (For a White Guy) • Self Esteem.

VOL. 33 – ACOUSTIC CLASSICS
00699656 / $14.95
Across the Universe • Babe, I'm Gonna Leave You • Crazy on You • Heart of Gold • Hotel California • I'd Love to Change the World • Thick As a Brick • Wanted Dead or Alive.

VOL. 34 – CLASSIC ROCK
00699658 / $14.95
Aqualung • Born to Be Wild • The Boys Are Back in Town • Brown Eyed Girl • Reeling in the Years • Rock'n Me • Rocky Mountain Way • Sweet Emotion.

VOL. 35 – HAIR METAL
00699660 / $14.95
Decadence Dance • Don't Treat Me Bad • Down Boys • Seventeen • Shake Me • Up All Night • Wait • Talk Dirty to Me.

VOL. 36 – SOUTHERN ROCK
00699661 / $14.95
Can't You See • Flirtin' with Disaster • Hold on Loosely • Jessica • Mississippi Queen • Ramblin' Man • Sweet Home Alabama • What's Your Name.

VOL. 37 – ACOUSTIC METAL
00699662 / $14.95
Every Rose Has Its Thorn • Fly to the Angels • Hole Hearted • Love Is on the Way • Love of a Lifetime • Signs • To Be with You • When the Children Cry.

VOL. 38 – BLUES
00699663 / $14.95
Boom Boom • Cold Shot • Crosscut Saw • Everyday I Have the Blues • Frosty • Further On up the Road • Killing Floor • Texas Flood.

VOL. 39 – '80S METAL
00699664 / $14.95
Bark at the Moon • Big City Nights • Breaking the Chains • Cult of Personality • Lay It Down • Living on a Prayer • Panama • Smokin' in the Boys Room.

VOL. 40 – INCUBUS
00699668 / $14.95
Are You In? • Drive • Megalomaniac • Nice to Know You • Pardon Me • Stellar • Talk Shows on Mute • Wish You Were Here.

VOL. 41 – ERIC CLAPTON
00699669 / $14.95
After Midnight • Can't Find My Way Home • Forever Man • I Shot the Sheriff • I'm Tore Down • Pretending • Running on Faith • Tears in Heaven.

VOL. 42 – CHART HITS
00699670 / $14.95
Are You Gonna Be My Girl • Heaven • Here Without You • I Believe in a Thing Called Love • Just Like You • Last Train Home • This Love • Until the Day I Die.

VOL. 43 – LYNYRD SKYNYRD
00699681 / $14.95
Don't Ask Me No Questions • Free Bird • Gimme Three Steps • I Know a Little • Saturday Night Special • Sweet Home Alabama • That Smell • You Got That Right.

VOL. 44 – JAZZ
00699689 / $14.95
I Remember You • I'll Remember April • Impressions • In a Mellow Tone • Moonlight in Vermont • On a Slow Boat to China • Things Ain't What They Used to Be • Yesterdays.

VOL. 46 – MAINSTREAM ROCK
00699722 / $14.95
Just a Girl • Keep Away • Kryptonite • Lightning Crashes • 1979 • One Step Closer • Scar Tissue • Torn.

VOL. 47 – HENDRIX SMASH HITS
00699723/ $16.95
All Along the Watchtower • Can You See Me? • Crosstown Traffic • Fire • Foxey Lady • Hey Joe • Manic Depression • Purple Haze • Red House • Remember • Stone Free • The Wind Cries Mary.

VOL. 48 – AEROSMITH CLASSICS
00699724 / $14.95
Back in the Saddle • Draw the Line • Dream On • Last Child • Mama Kin • Same Old Song & Dance • Sweet Emotion • Walk This Way.

VOL. 50 – NÜ METAL
00699726 / $14.95
Duality • Here to Stay • In the End • Judith • Nookie • So Cold • Toxicity • Whatever.

VOL. 51 – ALTERNATIVE '90S
00699727 / $14.95
Alive • Cherub Rock • Come As You Are • Give It Away • Jane Says • No Excuses • No Rain • Santeria.

VOL. 56 – FOO FIGHTERS
00699749 / $14.95
All My Life • Best of You • DOA • I'll Stick Around • Learn to Fly • Monkey Wrench • My Hero • This Is a Call.

VOL. 57 – SYSTEM OF A DOWN
00699751 / $14.95
Aerials • B.Y.O.B. • Chop Suey! • Innervision • Question! • Spiders • Sugar • Toxicity.

Prices, contents, and availability subject to change without notice.

FOR MORE INFORMATION, SEE YOUR LOCAL MUSIC DEALER, OR WRITE TO:

HAL•LEONARD® CORPORATION
7777 W. BLUEMOUND RD. P.O. BOX 13819 MILWAUKEE, WI 53213

Visit Hal Leonard online at www.halleonard.com

0106